JINGLE

SECTION

Jingle Section

Jingle 1: Noun Jingle

This little noun
Floating around
Names a person, place, or thing.
With a knick knack, paddy wack,
These are English rules.
Isn't language fun and cool?

Jingle 2: Verb Jingle

A verb, a verb. What is a verb?
Haven't you heard?
There are two kinds of verbs:
The action verb and the linking verb.

The action verb shows a state of action,
Like **stand** and **sit** and **smile**.
The action verb is always doing
Because it tells what the subject does.
We **stand**! We **sit**! We **smile**!

The linking verb is a state of being,
Like **am, is, are, was**, and **were**,
Looks, becomes, grows, and **feels**.
A linking verb shows no action
Because it tells what the subject is.
He **is** *a clown.*
He **looks** *funny.*

Jingle 3: Sentence Jingle

A sentence, sentence, sentence
Is complete, complete, complete
When 5 simple rules
It meets, meets, meets.

It has a subject, subject, subject
And a verb, verb, verb.
It makes sense, sense, sense
With every word, word, word.

Add a capital letter, letter
And an end mark, mark.
Now, we're finished, and aren't we smart!
Now, our sentence has all its parts!

REMEMBER
Subject, Verb, Com-plete sense,
Capital letter, and an end mark, too.
That's what a sentence is all about!

SHURLEY ENGLISH

HOMESCHOOL MADE EASY

LEVEL 4

Student Book

By

Brenda Shurley

Shurley Instructional Materials, Inc., Cabot, Arkansas

10-09
ISBN 978-1-58561-037-2 (Level 4 Student Workbook)

Shurley
Instructional
Materials, Inc.

Printed in the United States of America by RR Donnelley, Owensville, MO.

For additional information or to place an order, write to: Shurley Instructional Materials, Inc.
366 SIM Drive
Cabot, AR 72023

1 2 3 4 5 6   09 07 05 04 03 01

Jingle Section

Jingle 4: Adverb Jingle

An adverb modifies a verb, adjective, or another adverb.
An adverb asks *How? When? Where?*
To find an adverb: **Go, Ask, Get**.
Where do I **go**? To a verb, adjective, or another adverb.
What do I **ask**? How? When? Where?
What do I **get**? An ADVERB! (Clap) (Clap)
That's what!

Jingle 5: Adjective Jingle

An adjective modifies a noun or pronoun.
An adjective asks *What kind? Which one? How many?*
To find an adjective: **Go, Ask, Get**.
Where do I **go**? To a noun or pronoun.
What do I **ask**? What kind? Which one? How many?
What do I **get**? An ADJECTIVE! (Clap) (Clap)
That's what!

Jingle 6: Article Adjective

We are the article adjectives,
Teeny, tiny adjectives:
A, AN, THE - A, AN, THE.

We are called article adjectives and noun markers;
We are memorized and used every day.
So, if you spot us, you can mark us
With the label A.

We are the article adjectives,
Teeny, tiny adjectives:
A, AN, THE - A, AN, THE.

Jingle Section

Jingle 7: Preposition Jingle

A PREP PREP PREPOSITION
Is a special group of words
That connects a
NOUN, NOUN, NOUN
Or a PRO, PRO, PRONOUN
To the rest of the sentence.

Jingle 8: Object of the Prep Jingle

Dum De Dum Dum!
An O-P is a N-O-U-N or a P-R-O
After the P-R-E-P
In a S-E-N-T-E-N-C-E.
Dum De Dum Dum - DONE!

Jingle 9: Preposition Flow Jingle

1. **Preposition, Preposition Starting with an A.**
(Fast)
aboard, about, above,
across, after, against,
(Slow)
along, among, around, at.

2. **Preposition, Preposition Starting with a B.**
(Fast)
before, behind, below,
beneath, beside, between,
(Slow)
beyond, but, by.

3. **Preposition, Preposition Starting with a D.**
down (slow & long),
during (snappy).

4. **Preposition, Preposition Don't go away.
Go to the middle
And see what we say.
E-F-I and L-N-O**
except, for, from,
in, inside, into,
like,
near, of, off,
on, out, outside, over.

5. **Preposition, Preposition Almost through.
Start with P and end with W.**
past, since, through,
throughout, to, toward,
under, underneath,
until, up, upon,
with, within, without.

6. **Preposition, Preposition Easy as can be.
We're all finished,
And aren't you pleased?
We've just recited
All 49 of these.**

Jingle 10: Pronoun Jingle

This little pronoun,
Floating around,
Takes the place of a little old noun.
With a knick knack, paddy wack,
These are English rules.
Isn't language fun and cool?

Jingle 11: Subject Pronoun Jingle

There are seven subject pronouns
That are easy as can be:
I and we,   (clap 2 times)
He and she,   (clap 2 times)
It and they and you. (clap 3 times)

Jingle Section

Jingle 12: Possessive Pronoun Jingle

There are seven possessive pronouns
That are easy as can be:
My and our,   (clap 2 times)
His and her,   (clap 2 times)
Its and their and your.   (clap 3 times)

Jingle 13: Object Pronoun Jingle

There are seven object pronouns
That are easy as can be:
Me and us,   (clap 2 times)
Him and her,   (clap 2 times)
It and them and you.   (clap 3 times)

Jingle 14:   The 23 Helping Verbs of the Mean, Lean Verb Machine Jingle

These 23 helping verbs will be on my test.
I gotta remember them so I can do my best.
I'll start out with 8 and finish with 15;
Just call me the mean, lean verb machine.

There are 8 *be* verbs that are easy as can be:
    am, is, are – was and were,
    am, is, are – was and were,
    am, is, are – was and were,
    be, being, and been.

All together now, the 8 *be* verbs:
am, is, are – was and were – be, being, and been.
am, is, are – was and were – be, being, and been.

There're 23 helping verbs, and I've recited only 8.
That leaves fifteen more that I must relate:
    has, have, and had – do, does, and did,
    has, have, and had – do, does, and did,
    might, must, may – might, must, may.

Knowing these verbs will save my grade:
    can and could – would and should,
    can and could – would and should,
    shall and will,
    shall and will.

In record time, I did this drill.
I'm the mean, lean verb machine - STILL!

Jingle 15:   Eight Parts of Speech Jingle

Want to know how to write?
Use the eight parts of speech - They're dynamite!

Nouns, **V**erbs, and **P**ronouns - They rule!
They're called the **NVP's**, and they're really cool!

The **Double A's** are on the move;
Adjectives and **A**dverbs help you groove!

Next come the **PIC's**, and then we're done!
The **PIC's** are **P**reposition, **I**nterjection, and **C**onjunction!

All together now, the eight parts of speech, abbreviations please:
NVP, AA, PIC   NVP, AA, PIC!

Jingle Section

Jingle 16:   Direct Object Jingle
1. A direct object is a noun or pronoun.
2. A direct object completes the meaning of the sentence.
3. A direct object is located after the verb-transitive
4. To find the direct object, ask WHAT or WHOM after your verb.

Jingle 17:   Indirect Object Jingle
1. An indirect object is a noun or pronoun.
2. An indirect object receives what the direct object names.
3. An indirect object is located between the verb-transitive and the direct object.
4. To find the indirect object, ask TO WHOM or FOR WHOM after the direct object.

REFERENCE

SECTION

Vocabulary Reference

Chapter 1, Vocabulary Words #1	Chapter 1, Vocabulary Words #2
(bold, timid, slumber, sleep)	(modest, forward, depart, leave)

Chapter 2, Vocabulary Words #1	Chapter 2, Vocabulary Words #2
(calamity, disaster, admire, detest)	(easy, complicated, precise, exact)

Chapter 3, Vocabulary Words #1	Chapter 3, Vocabulary Words #2
(idle, busy, hinted, implied)	(quiver, shake, aggression, retreat)

Chapter 4, Vocabulary Words #1	Chapter 4, Vocabulary Words #2
(reply, answer, vivid, dingy)	(muscle, brawn, delight, displease)

Chapter 5, Vocabulary Words #1	Chapter 5, Vocabulary Words #2
(accept, reject, tales, stories)	(pursue, follow, proceed, cease)

Chapter 6, Vocabulary Words #1	Chapter 6, Vocabulary Words #2
(soiled, dirty, calm, turmoil)	(arrange, prepare, encourage, belittle)

Chapter 7, Vocabulary Words #1	Chapter 7, Vocabulary Words #2
(rival, competitor, fatigued, fresh)	(uplift, depress, pail, bucket)

Chapter 8, Vocabulary Words #1	Chapter 8, Vocabulary Words #2
(unique, common, promise, pledge)	(keen, sharp, impetuous, cautious)

Chapter 9, Vocabulary Words #1	Chapter 9, Vocabulary Words #2
(quill, feather, rip, mend)	(hardy, robust, creeping, rushing)

Chapter 10, Vocabulary Words #1	Chapter 10, Vocabulary Words #2
(complex, difficult, petite, large)	(finish, commence, rude, impolite)

Chapter 11, Vocabulary Words #1	Chapter 11, Vocabulary Words #2
(fable, fiction, logical, silly)	(hesitate, pause, auction, buy)

Vocabulary Reference

Chapter 12, Vocabulary Words #1	Chapter 12, Vocabulary Words #2
(demand, suggest, endow, give)	(quick, agile, begins, originates)

Chapter 13, Vocabulary Words #1	Chapter 13, Vocabulary Words #2
(conceal, hide, fake, genuine)	(adhere, stick, gallant, afraid)

Chapter 14, Vocabulary Words #1	Chapter 14, Vocabulary Words #2
(emerge, disappear, shy, bashful)	(treaty, agreement, flashy, plain)

Chapter 15, Vocabulary Words #1	Chapter 15, Vocabulary Words #2
(delicious, tasty, approve, deplore)	(hope, despair, influence, sway)

Chapter 16, Vocabulary Words #1	Chapter 16, Vocabulary Words #2
(mock, mimic, drought, flood)	(nervous, uneasy, important, petty)

Chapter 17, Vocabulary Words #1	Chapter 17, Vocabulary Words #2
(praise, commend, flimsy, sturdy)	(neutral, biased, young, youth)

Chapter 18, Vocabulary Words #1	Chapter 18, Vocabulary Words #2
(escalate, decrease, danger, peril)	(bicker, agree, error, wrong)

Chapter 19, Vocabulary Words #1	Chapter 19, Vocabulary Words #2
(remain, stay, dim, bright)	(connect, separate, puzzle, mystery)

Chapter 20, Vocabulary Words #1	Chapter 20, Vocabulary Words #2
(dwell, live, subordinate, leader)	(mistake, blunder, allow, forbid)

Chapter 21, Vocabulary Words #1	Chapter 21, Vocabulary Words #2
(terror, fear, compete, cooperate)	(safe, secure, clutter, order)

Chapter 22, Vocabulary Words #1	Chapter 22, Vocabulary Words #2
(stern, hard, harshness, sweetness)	(innocent, guilty, remember, retain)

Reference 1: Beginning Setup Plan for Homeschool

You should use this plan to keep things in order!

1. Have separate color-coded pocket folders for each subject.
2. Put unfinished work in the right-hand side and finished work in the left-hand side of each subject folder.
3. Put notes to study, graded tests, and study guides in the brads so you will have them to study for scheduled tests.
4. Have a paper folder to store clean sheets of paper. Keep it full at all times.
5. Have an assignment folder to be reviewed every day.

Things to keep in your assignment folder:

A. Keep a monthly calendar of assignments, test dates, report-due dates, project-due dates, extra activities, dates and times, review dates, etc.

B. Keep a grade sheet to record the grades received in each subject. (*You might also consider keeping your grades on the inside cover of each subject folder. However you keep your grades, just remember to record them accurately. Your grades are your business, so keep up with them! Grades help you know which areas need attention.*)

C. Make a list every day of the things you want to do so you can keep track of what you finish and what you have not finished. Move the unfinished items to your new list the next day. (*Making this list takes time, but it's your road map to success. You will always know at a glance what you set out to accomplish and what still needs to be done.*)

6. Keep all necessary school supplies in a handy, heavy-duty Ziploc bag or a pencil bag.

Reference 2: Synonyms, Antonyms, and Five-Step Vocabulary Plan

Part 1: Synonyms and Antonyms

Definitions: Synonyms are words that have similar, or almost the same, meanings. Antonyms are words that have opposite meanings.

Directions: Identify each pair of words as synonyms or antonyms by putting parentheses ( ) around **syn** or **ant**.

1. bashful, shy **(syn)** ant   2. reply, answer **(syn)** ant   3. absent, present syn **(ant)**

Part 2: Five-Step Vocabulary Plan

(1) Write a title for the vocabulary words in each chapter.
Example: **Chapter 1, Vocabulary Words**

(2) Write each vocabulary word in your vocabulary notebook.

(3) Look up each vocabulary word in a dictionary or thesaurus.

(4) Write the meaning beside each vocabulary word.

(5) Write a sentence that helps you remember how each vocabulary word is used.

Reference 3: A and An Choices

Rule 1: Use the word *a* when the next word begins with a consonant sound. (*Example: a red apple.*)

Rule 2: Use the word *an* when the next word begins with a vowel sound. (*Example: an apple.*)

Example Sentences: Write *a* or *an* in the blanks.

1. Would you like ___**an**___ angel necklace?   3. We saw ___**a**___ statue in the courtyard.

2. Would you like ___**a**___ gold angel necklace?   4. I saw ___**an**___ old statue in the courtyard.

Reference 4: What is Journal Writing?

Journal Writing is a written record of your personal thoughts and feelings about things or people that are important to you. Recording your thoughts in a journal is a good way to remember how you felt about what was happening in your life at a particular time. You can record your dreams, memories, feelings, and experiences. You can ask questions and answer some of them. It is fun to go back later and read what you have written because it shows how you have changed in different areas of your life. A journal can also be an excellent place to look for future writing topics, creative stories, poems, etc. Writing in a journal is an easy and enjoyable way to practice your writing skills without worrying about a writing grade.

What do I write about?

Journals are personal, but sometimes it helps to have ideas to get you started. Remember, in a journal, you do not have to stick to one topic. Write about someone or something you like. Write about what you did last weekend or on vacation. Write about what you hope to do this week or on your next vacation. Write about home, school, friends, hobbies, special talents (yours or someone else's), or present and future hopes and fears. Write about what is wrong in your world and what you would do to "fix" it. Write about the good things and the bad things in your world. If you think about a past event and want to write an opinion about it now, put it in your journal. If you want to give your opinion about a present or future event that could have an impact on your life or the way that you see things, put it in your journal. If something bothers you, record it in your journal. If something interests you, record it. If you just want to record something that doesn't seem important at all, write it in your journal. After all, it is your journal!

How do I get started writing in my personal journal?

You need to put the day's date on the title line of your paper: **Month, Day, Year.** Skip the next line and begin your entry. You might write one or two sentences, a paragraph, a whole page, or several pages. Except for the journal date, no particular organizational style is required for journal writing. You decide how best to organize and express your thoughts. Feel free to include sketches, diagrams, lists, etc., if they will help you remember your thoughts about a topic or an event. You will also need a spiral notebook, a pen, a quiet place, and at least 5-10 minutes of uninterrupted writing time.

Note: Use a pen if possible. Pencils have lead points that break, and erasers, both of which slow down your thoughts. Any drawings you might include do not have to be masterpieces—stick figures will do nicely.

Reference 5: Checklists

Revision Checklist

1. Eliminate unnecessary or needlessly repeated words or ideas.
2. Combine or reorder sentences.
3. Change word choices for clarity and expression.
4. Know the purpose: to explain, to describe, to entertain, or to persuade.
5. Know the audience: the reader(s) of the writing.

Beginning Editing Checklist

1. Did you indent the paragraph?
2. Did you capitalize the first word and put an end mark at the end of every sentence?
3. Did you spell words correctly?

More Editing Skills

4. Did you follow the writing guidelines? (*Reference 13, page 17*)
5. Did you list the topic and three points on separate lines at the top of the paper?
6. Did you follow the three-point paragraph pattern?
7. Did you write in the point of view assigned? (*first or third person*)
8. Did you use the correct homonyms?
9. Did you follow all other capitalization and punctuation rules?
10. Did you follow the three-paragraph essay pattern?

Final Paper Checklist

1. Have you written the correct heading on your paper?
2. Have you written your final paper in ink?
3. Have you single-spaced your final paper?
4. Have you written your final paper neatly?
5. Have you stapled the final paper to the rough draft and handed them in to your teacher?

Writing Process Checklist

1. Gather information.
2. Write a rough draft.
3. Revise the rough draft.
4. Edit the rough draft.
5. Write a final paper.

Reference 6: Rough Drafts and Final Paragraph

Rough Draft

When Melissa arrived, at the airport last weak, the terminial were so conjested that she could hardly move. Melissa quickly moved through the airports crowded hallways, because she was already late. She arrived at the right terminial just in time to bored her flight. Melissa was out of breath and her hart was beating hard too. When she reached her seat on the plain, she was tired. Before she fell asleep she promised to allow extra time on the next trip for the large crowds.

Revision of Draft

When Melissa arrived, at the airport last weak, the terminial were so conjested she could **barely** move. **Because she was already late, Melissa rushed through the airports crowded corridors.** She arrived at the **correct** terminial just in time to bored her flight. Melissa was out of breath and **her hart was pounding rapidly from her mad dash through the airport**. When she **finally** reached her seat on the plain, she was **exhausted**. Before she fell asleep she promised **herself that on the next trip, she would allow extra time for the enormous crowds at the airport.**

Edit Draft

When Melissa arrived [**delete comma**] at the airport last week, [*week*, **not** *weak*] the terminal [**terminal, not** *terminial*] was [*was*, **not** *were*] so congested [**congested, not conjested**] she could barely move. Because she was already late, Melissa rushed through the airport's [**apostrophe added**] crowded corridors. She arrived at the correct terminal [*terminal*, **not** *terminial*] just in time to board [*board*, **not** *bored*] her flight. Melissa was out of breath, [**comma inserted**] and her heart [*heart*, **not** *hart*] was pounding rapidly from her mad dash through the airport. When she finally reached her seat on the plane [*plane*, **not** *plain*], she was exhausted. Before she fell asleep, [**comma inserted**] she promised herself that on the next trip, she would allow extra time for the enormous crowds at the airport.

Final Paragraph

When Melissa arrived at the airport last week, the terminal was so congested she could barely move. Because she was already late, Melissa rushed through the airport's crowded corridors. She arrived at the correct terminal just in time to board her flight. Melissa was out of breath, and her heart was pounding rapidly from her mad dash through the airport. When she finally reached her seat on the plane, she was exhausted. Before she fell asleep, she promised herself that on the next trip, she would allow extra time for the enormous crowds at the airport.

Reference 7: The Four Kinds of Sentences and the End Mark Flow

1. A **declarative** sentence makes a statement. It is labeled with a **D**.
   Example: Lisa bought a video.
   (Period, statement, declarative sentence)

2. An **imperative** sentence gives a command. It is labeled with an **Imp**.
   Example: Take the mail to the post office.
   (Period, command, imperative sentence)

3. An **interrogative** sentence asks a question. It is labeled with an **Int**.
   Example: What is in your lunch box?
   (Question mark, question, interrogative sentence)

4. An **exclamatory** sentence expresses strong feeling. It is labeled with an **E**.
   Example: The roller coaster is awesome!
   (Exclamation point, strong feeling, exclamatory sentence)

Examples: Read each sentence, recite the end-mark flow in parentheses, and put the end mark and the abbreviation for the sentence type in the blank at the end of each sentence.

1. Monday is a holiday **. D**
   (Period, statement, declarative sentence)

2. The car rolled down the street **! E**
   (Exclamation point, strong feeling, exclamatory sentence)

3. Peel the apples in the kitchen **. Imp**
   (Period, command, imperative sentence)

4. Will your mother be home tonight **? Int**
   (Question mark, question, interrogative sentence)

Reference 8: Additional Article Adjective Information

1. **A/An** are called <u>indefinite</u> articles, meaning one of several.
   (Examples: **a** brown cow—**an** arrow.)

2. **The** is called a <u>definite</u> article, meaning there is only one.
   (Examples: **the** brown cow—**the** arrow.)

3. The article **The** has two pronunciations:

   a. As a long **e** (*where the article precedes a word that begins with a vowel sound: the elbow, the infant*)

   b. As a short **u** (*where the article precedes a word that begins with a consonant sound: the book, the tree*)

Reference 9: Question and Answer Flow Sentence

Question and Answer Flow for Sentence 1: The excited little girl cheered very loudly.

1. Who cheered very loudly? girl - SN
2. What is being said about girl? girl cheered - V
3. Cheered how? loudly - Adv
4. How loudly? very - Adv
5. What kind of girl? little - Adj
6. What kind of girl? excited - Adj
7. The - A
8. SN V P1 Check
9. Period, statement, declarative sentence
10. Go back to the verb - divide the complete subject from the complete predicate.

Classified Sentence:

```
                       A    Adj  Adj SN    V    Adv  Adv
          SN   V     The excited little girl / cheered very loudly.  D
          P1
```

Reference 10: Definitions for a Skill Builder Check

1. A **noun** names a person, place, or thing.

2. A **singular noun** usually does not end in an *s* or *es* and means only one. (*book, flower, shoe*)
   Underline{Exception}: Some nouns end in s and are singular and mean only one. (*recess, dress*)

3. A **plural noun** usually ends in an *s* or *es* and means more than one. (*books, flowers, shoes*)
   Underline{Exception}: Some nouns are made plural by changing their spelling. (*woman-women, child-children*)

4. A **common noun** names ANY person, place, or thing. A common noun is not capitalized because it does not name a specific person, place, or thing. (*watch, purse*)

5. A **proper noun** is a noun that names a specific, or particular, person, place, or thing. Proper nouns are always capitalized no matter where they are located in the sentence. (*David, Texas*)

6. A **simple subject** is another name for the subject noun or subject pronoun.

7. A **simple predicate** is another name for the verb.

Reference 11: Noun Job Chart

Directions: Classify the sentence below. Underline the complete subject once and the complete predicate twice. Then, complete the table.

```
           A   Adj   SN      V    Adv   Adv
SN V       The happy children / played quietly today.  D
P1
```

List the Noun Used	List the Noun Job	Singular or Plural	Common or Proper	Simple Subject	Simple Predicate
children	SN	P	C	children	played

Reference 12: Three-Point Paragraph Example

Topic: **My favorite subjects**

Three main points: 1. **geography**   2. **English**   3. **science**

Sentence #1 – <u>Topic Sentence</u> (*Use words in the topic and tell how many points will be used.*)
I have three favorite subjects.

Sentence #2 – <u>3-Point Sentence</u> (*List the 3 points in the order you will present them.*)
These subjects are geography, English, and science.

Sentence #3 – <u>First Point</u>
My first favorite subject is geography.

Sentence #4 – <u>Supporting Sentence</u> for the first point.
I like geography because it lets me travel to countries all over the world.

Sentence #5 – <u>Second Point</u>
My second favorite subject is English.

Sentence #6 – <u>Supporting Sentence</u> for the second point.
I especially enjoy the opportunity to write stories and be creative.

Sentence #7 – <u>Third Point</u>
My third favorite subject is science.

Sentence #8 – <u>Supporting Sentence</u> for the third point.
I love science because I get to study creatures of all kinds.

Sentence #9 – <u>Concluding (final) Sentence</u> (*Restate the topic sentence and add an extra thought.*)
I enjoy studying all kinds of subjects, but my favorites will probably always be geography, English, and science.

SAMPLE PARAGRAPH

My Favorite Subjects

   I have three favorite subjects. These subjects are geography, English, and science. My first favorite subject is geography. I like geography because it lets me travel to countries all over the world. My second favorite subject is English. I especially enjoy the opportunity to write stories and be creative. My third favorite subject is science. I love science because I get to study creatures of all kinds. I enjoy studying all kinds of subjects, but my favorites will probably always be geography, English, and science.

Reference 13: Writing Guidelines

1. Label your writing assignment in the top right-hand corner of your page with the following information:
   A. Your Name
   B. The Writing Assignment Number. *(Example: WA#1, WA#2, etc.)*
   C. Type of Writing *(Examples: Expository Paragraph, Persuasive Essay, Descriptive Paragraph, etc.)*
   D. The title of the writing on the top of the first line.

2. Think about the topic that you are assigned.

3. Think about the type of writing assigned, which is the purpose for the writing.
   (Is your writing intended to explain, persuade, describe, or narrate?)

4. Think about the writing format, which is the organizational plan you are expected to use.
   (Is your assignment a paragraph, a 3-paragraph essay, a 5-paragraph essay, or a letter?)

5. Use your writing time wisely.
   (Begin work quickly and concentrate on your assignment until it is finished.)

Reference 14: Predicate Words Located in the Complete Subject

1. An adverb at the beginning of the sentence will modify the verb.
   (Example: <u>Yesterday</u>, <u>we</u> / <u>went to the park</u>.) (<u>We</u> / <u>went to the park yesterday</u>.)

2. A helping verb at the beginning of a sentence will always be part of the verb.
   (Example: <u>Are</u> <u>we</u> / <u>going to the park</u>?) (<u>We</u> / <u>are going to the park</u>.)

3. A prepositional phrase at the beginning of a sentence will modify the verb.
   (Example: <u>At the park</u>, <u>we</u> / <u>played with the children</u>.) (<u>We</u> / <u>played with the children at the park</u>.)

To add *predicate words in the complete subject* to the Question and Answer Flow, say, "*This sentence has predicate words in the complete subject. Underline the (adverb), (helping verb), or (prepositional phrase) twice.*" If there are no predicate words in the complete subject, then you will not do this step.

Reference 15: Practice Sentence

Labels:	A	Adj	Adj	SN	V	Adv	Adv
Practice:	**The**	**harmless**	**little**	**insect**	**crawled**	**quietly**	**away.**

Reference 16: Improved Sentence

Labels:	A	Adj	Adj	SN	V	Adv	Adv
Practice:	The	harmless	little	insect	crawled	quietly	away.
Improved:	**An**	**innocent**	**red**	**ladybug**	**scurried**	**frantically**	**around.**
	(word change)	(synonym)	(word change)	(synonym)	(synonym)	(antonym)	(word change)

Reference 17: Knowing the Difference Between Prepositions and Adverbs

Adv

In the sample sentence, *Susan fell* **down**, the word **down** is an adverb because it does not have a noun after it.

P   noun (OP)

In the sample sentence, *Susan fell* **down the stairs**, the word **down** is a preposition because it has the noun **stairs** (the object of the preposition) after it. To find the preposition and object of the preposition in the Question and Answer Flow, say:

    down – P   (Say: *down – preposition*)

    down what? stairs – OP   (Say: *down what? stairs – object of the preposition*)

Reference 18: Writing in First Person or Third Person

Events and stories can be told from different viewpoints.

First Person Point of View uses the first person pronouns *I, we, us, me, my, mine, our*, and *ours* to name the speaker. If any of the first person pronouns are used in a writing, the writing is usually considered a first person writing, even though second and third person pronouns may also be used. First person shows that you (*the writer*) are speaking, and that you (*the writer*) are personally involved in what is happening.

(Examples: **I** am going to the store in **my** new car. She likes **my** car.)

Third Person Point of View uses the third person pronouns *he, his, him, she, her, hers, it, its, they, their, theirs*, and *them* to name the person or thing spoken about. You should <u>not</u> use the first person pronouns *I, we, us, me, my, mine, our* and *ours* for third person writing because using the first person pronouns usually puts a writing in a first person point of view. Third person means that you (*the writer*) must write as if you are watching the events take place. Third person shows that you are writing about another person, thing, or event.

(Examples: **He** is going to the store in **his** new car. **She** likes **his** car.)

Reference 19: Subject Pronoun

1. A **subject pronoun** takes the place of a noun that is used as the subject of a sentence.

2. These are the most common subject pronouns: *I, we, he, she, it, they*, and *you*.
   Use the Subject Pronoun Jingle to remember the common subject pronouns.

3. To find a subject pronoun, ask the subject question *who* or *what*.

4. Label a subject pronoun with an **SP**.

5. Call the **SP** abbreviation a subject pronoun.

Reference 20: Understood Subject Pronoun

1. A sentence has an **understood subject** when someone gives a command or makes a request and leaves the subject unwritten or unspoken. It is understood that the unspoken subject will always be the pronoun *you*.

2. An imperative sentence gives a command or makes a request. It ends with a period or an exclamation point and always has the word *you* understood, but not expressed, as the subject.

3. The understood subject pronoun *you* is always written in parentheses at the beginning of the sentence with the label **SP** beside or above it: **(You) SP**.

4. Call the abbreviation **(You) SP** an understood subject pronoun.

Reference 21: Possessive Pronouns

1. A possessive pronoun takes the place of a possessive noun.

2. A possessive pronoun's spelling form makes it possessive. These are the most common possessive pronouns: *my, our, his, her, its, their,* and *your.* Use the Possessive Pronoun Jingle to remember the most common possessive pronouns.

3. A possessive pronoun has two jobs: to show ownership or possession and to modify like an adjective.

4. When classifying a possessive pronoun, both jobs will be recognized by labeling it as a possessive pronoun adjective. Use the abbreviation **PPA** (possessive pronoun adjective).

5. Include possessive pronouns when you are asked to identify pronouns, possessives, or adjectives.

6. To find a possessive pronoun, begin with the question *whose*. (*Whose book? His - PPA*)

Reference 22: Subject-Verb Agreement Rules

Rule 1: A singular subject must use a singular verb form that ends in **s**: *is, was, has, does, or verbs ending with* **es**.

Rule 2: A plural subject, a compound subject, or the subject **YOU** must use a plural verb form that has **no s** ending: *are, were, do, have, or verbs without* **s** *or* **es** *endings*. (A plural verb form is also called the *plain form.*)

Examples: For each sentence, do these four things: (1) Write the subject. (2) Write **S** if the subject is singular or **P** if the subject is plural. (3) Write the rule number. (4) Underline the correct verb in the sentence.

Subject	S or P	Rule	
book	S	1	1. The **book** (<u>was</u>, were) on the kitchen table.
cake and **pie**	P	2	2. **Cake** and **pie** (is, <u>are</u>) popular desserts.
You	P	2	3. **You** (cooks, <u>cook</u>) supper tonight.

Reference 23: Singular and Plural Points

Three-Point Expository Paragraph in First Person

Topic: My favorite books
3-points: 1. mysteries   2. spy novels   3. autobiographies

    I have three favorite books. These books are mysteries, spy novels, and autobiographies. My first favorite book is a mystery. I love mysteries because they are suspenseful and fun to read. My second favorite book is a spy novel. I like spy novels because they are exciting and adventurous. My third favorite book is an autobiography. I enjoy reading autobiographies because I like reading about famous people. My three favorite books are entertaining, and I enjoy reading them as much as I can.

Three-Point Expository Paragraph in Third Person

Topic: Emily's favorite books
3-points: 1. mysteries   2. spy novels   3. autobiographies

    Emily has three favorite books. These books are mysteries, spy novels, and autobiographies. Emily's first favorite book is a mystery. She loves mysteries because they are suspenseful and fun to read. Emily's second favorite book is a spy novel. She likes spy novels because they are exciting and adventurous. Emily's third favorite book is an autobiography. She enjoys reading autobiographies because she likes reading about famous people. Emily's three favorite books are entertaining, and she enjoys reading them as much as she can.

Reference 24: Possessive Nouns

1. A possessive noun is the name of a person, place, or thing that owns something.

2. A possessive noun will always have an apostrophe after it. It will be either an *apostrophe s* (*'s*) or an *s apostrophe* (*s'*). The apostrophe makes a noun show ownership. (*Mitchell's scooter*)

3. A possessive noun has two jobs: to show ownership or possession and to modify like an adjective.

4. When classifying a possessive noun, both jobs will be recognized by labeling it as a possessive noun adjective. Use the abbreviation **PNA** (possessive noun adjective).

5. Include possessive nouns when you are asked to identify possessive nouns or adjectives. Do not include possessive nouns when you are asked to identify regular nouns.

6. To find a possessive noun, begin with the question *whose*. (*Whose scooter? Mitchell's - PNA*)

Reference 25: Object Pronoun

1. If a pronoun does any job that has the word *object* in it, that pronoun is an object pronoun. Object pronouns can be used as objects of the prepositions, direct objects, or indirect objects.

2. The object pronouns are listed in your Object Pronoun Jingle:
   me, us, him, her, it, them, and *you.*

3. An object pronoun does not have a special label. An object pronoun keeps the **OP**, **DO**, or **IO** label that tells its job.

	OP	**DO**	**IO**
Examples:	Lisa left with *her.*	My mother called *me.*	Mail *him* the letter.

Reference 26A: Paragraphs Using Different Writing Forms

Topic: My favorite snacks **3-points:** 1. ice cream   2. popcorn   3. peanut butter crackers

Sample 1: Three-point paragraph, using a standard topic sentence with time-order points

   I have three favorite snacks. They are ice cream, popcorn, and peanut butter crackers. **First**, I like ice cream. I like all the different flavors of ice cream, and I laugh when the cold tickles my tongue. **Second**, I like popcorn. To me popcorn is best when it is hot and covered with lots of melted butter. **Third**, I like peanut butter crackers. (*or* **Finally**, *I like peanut butter crackers.*) I like peanut butter crackers because they are so fun to make. I enjoy many different snacks, but my favorites will always be ice cream, popcorn, and peanut butter crackers.

Sample 2: Three-point paragraph, using a standard topic sentence with different time-order points

   I have three favorite snacks. They are ice cream, popcorn, and peanut butter crackers. **First**, I like ice cream. I like all the different flavors of ice cream, and I laugh when the cold tickles my tongue. **Next**, I like popcorn. To me, popcorn is best when it is hot and covered with lots of melted butter. **Last**, I like peanut butter crackers. (*or* **Finally**, *I like peanut butter crackers.*) I like peanut butter crackers because they are so fun to make. I enjoy many different snacks, but my favorites will always be ice cream, popcorn, and peanut butter crackers.

Reference 26B: Paragraphs Using Different Writing Forms

Sample 3: Three-point paragraph using a general topic sentence with standard points

I enjoy the county fair for many reasons. Three of these reasons are livestock judging, riding the Ferris wheel, and eating cotton candy. My first reason for enjoying the county fair is the livestock judging. I enjoy showing my prize bull in the judge's ring before dozens of my friends. My second reason for enjoying the county fair is riding the Ferris wheel. I especially like the thrill of coming down fast and getting that hollow feeling in my stomach. My third reason for enjoying the county fair is eating cotton candy. I love its sticky texture and getting it all over my fingers and hands. Given the fact that the fair comes but once a year, I make the most of enjoying it for these three reasons.

Sample 4: Three-point paragraph using a general topic sentence with time-order points

I enjoy the county fair for many reasons. Three of these reasons are livestock judging, riding the Ferris wheel, and eating cotton candy. First, I enjoy the county fair for the livestock judging. I enjoy showing my prize bull in the judge's ring before dozens of my friends. Next, I enjoy the county fair for riding the Ferris wheel. I especially like the thrill of coming down fast and getting that hollow feeling in my stomach. Last, I enjoy the county fair because I love to eat cotton candy. (or Finally, *I enjoy the county fair because I love to eat cotton candy.*) I love its sticky texture and getting it all over my fingers and hands. Given the fact that the fair comes but once a year, I make the most of enjoying it for these three reasons.

Reference 27: Irregular Verb Chart

PRESENT	PAST	PAST PARTICIPLE		PRESENT PARTICIPLE	
become	became	(has)	become	(is)	becoming
blow	blew	(has)	blown	(is)	blowing
break	broke	(has)	broken	(is)	breaking
bring	brought	(has)	brought	(is)	bringing
burst	burst	(has)	burst	(is)	bursting
buy	bought	(has)	bought	(is)	buying
choose	chose	(has)	chosen	(is)	choosing
come	came	(has)	come	(is)	coming
drink	drank	(has)	drunk	(is)	drinking
drive	drove	(has)	driven	(is)	driving
eat	ate	(has)	eaten	(is)	eating
fall	fell	(has)	fallen	(is)	falling
fly	flew	(has)	flown	(is)	flying
freeze	froze	(has)	frozen	(is)	freezing
get	got	(has)	gotten	(is)	getting
give	gave	(has)	given	(is)	giving
grow	grew	(has)	grown	(is)	growing
know	knew	(has)	known	(is)	knowing
lie	lay	(has)	lain	(is)	lying
lay	laid	(has)	laid	(is)	laying
make	made	(has)	made	(is)	making
ride	rode	(has)	ridden	(is)	riding
ring	rang	(has)	rung	(is)	ringing
rise	rose	(has)	risen	(is)	rising
sell	sold	(has)	sold	(is)	selling
sing	sang	(has)	sung	(is)	singing
sink	sank	(has)	sunk	(is)	sinking
set	set	(has)	set	(is)	setting
sit	sat	(has)	sat	(is)	sitting
shoot	shot	(has)	shot	(is)	shooting
swim	swam	(has)	swum	(is)	swimming
take	took	(has)	taken	(is)	taking
tell	told	(has)	told	(is)	telling
throw	threw	(has)	thrown	(is)	throwing
wear	wore	(has)	worn	(is)	wearing
write	wrote	(has)	written	(is)	writing

Reference 28: Homonym Chart

Homonyms are words that sound the same but have different meanings and different spellings.

1. **capital** - upper part, main	15. **lead** - metal	29. **their** - belonging to them
2. **capitol** - statehouse	16. **led** - guided	30. **there** - in that place
3. **coarse** - rough	17. **no** - not so	31. **they're** - they are
4. **course** - route	18. **know** - to understand	32. **threw** - did throw
5. **council** - assembly	19. **right** - correct	33. **through** - from end to end
6. **counsel** - advice	20. **write** - to form letters	34. **to** - toward, preposition
7. **forth** - forward	21. **principle** - a truth/rule/law	35. **too** - denoting excess
8. **fourth** - ordinal number	22. **principal** - chief/head person	36. **two** - a couple
9. **its** - possessive pronoun	23. **stationary** - motionless	37. **your** - belonging to you
10. **it's** - it is	24. **stationery** - paper	38. **you're** - you are
11. **hear** - to listen	25. **peace** - quiet	39. **weak** - not strong
12. **here** - in this place	26. **piece** - a part	40. **week** - seven days
13. **knew** - understood	27. **sent** - caused to go	41. **days** - more than one day
14. **new** - not old	28. **scent** - odor	42. **daze** - a confused state

Directions: Underline the correct homonym.

1. Mr. Davis is a member of the church (counsel, **council**).
2. Mr. and Mrs. Smith give (council, **counsel**) to troubled teenagers.

Reference 29: Three-Point Paragraph and Essay

Outline of a Three-Point Paragraph

I. Title

II. Paragraph   (9 sentences)

   A. Topic sentence

   B. A three-point sentence

   C. A **first-point** sentence

   D. A **supporting** sentence for the first point

   E. A **second-point** sentence

   F. A **supporting** sentence
     for the second point

   G. A **third-point** sentence

   H. A **supporting** sentence for the third point

   I. A concluding sentence

Outline of a Three-Paragraph Essay

I. Title

II. Paragraph 1 – Introduction   (3 sentences)

   A. Topic and general number sentence

   B. Extra information about the topic sentence

   C. Three-point sentence

III. Paragraph 2 – Body   (6-9 sentences)

   A. **First-point** sentence

   B. One or two **supporting** sentences for the first point

   C. **Second-point** sentence

   D. One or two **supporting** sentences for the second point

   E. **Third-point** sentence

   F. One or two **supporting** sentences for the third point

IV. Paragraph 3 – Conclusion   (2 sentences)

   A. Concluding general statement

   B. Concluding summary sentence

Reference 30: Steps in Writing a Three-Paragraph Expository Essay

WRITING TOPIC: Playing a Musical Instrument

LIST THE POINTS FOR THE TOPIC

◆ Select three points to list about the topic.
1. **Opens the door to a new world of art**
2. **Teaches self-discipline**
3. **Creates lifelong enjoyment of music**

WRITING THE INTRODUCTION AND TITLE

1. Sentence #1 - Topic Sentence
   Write the topic sentence by using the words in your topic and adding a general number word, such as *several, many, some*, or *numerous*, instead of the exact number of points you will discuss.
   (I have discovered that playing a musical instrument can provide many opportunities for people who love music.)

2. Sentence #2 - Extra Information about the topic sentence
   This sentence can clarify, explain, define, or just be an extra interesting comment about the topic sentence. If you need another sentence to complete your information, write an extra sentence here. If you write an extra sentence, your introductory paragraph will have four sentences in it instead of three.
   (Although many people focus solely on developing sports-related abilities, I think musical talents are just as important to develop.)

3. Sentence #3 - Three-point sentence
   This sentence will list the three points to be discussed in the order that you will present them in the body of your paper. You can list the points with or without the specific number in front.
   (Playing a musical instrument opens the door to a new world of art, teaches self-discipline, and creates a lifelong enjoyment of music.) or **(The three reasons why I enjoy playing a musical instrument are that it opens the door to a new world of art, teaches self-discipline, and creates a lifelong enjoyment of music.)**

◆ The Title - Since there are many possibilities for titles, look at the topic and the three points listed about the topic. Use some of the words in the topic and write a phrase to tell what your paragraph is about. Your title can be short or long. Capitalize the first, last, and important words in your title.
   (The Benefits of Playing a Musical Instrument)

WRITING THE BODY

4. Sentence #4 - First Point - Write a sentence stating your first point.
   (One of the reasons I enjoy playing a musical instrument is that it opens the door to a new world of art.)

5. Sentence #5 - Supporting Sentence(s) - Write one or two sentences that give more information about your first point.
   (In learning to play different pieces of music on an instrument, one explores a wide range of artistic styles.)

Reference 30: Steps in Writing a Three-Paragraph Expository Essay (continued)

6. <u>Sentence #6 - Second Point</u> - Write a sentence stating your second point. **(Another reason I enjoy playing a musical instrument is that it teaches self-discipline.)**

7. <u>Sentence #7 - Supporting Sentence(s)</u> - Write one or two sentences that give more information about your second point. **(Without a doubt, it requires devotion to the instrument.)**

8. <u>Sentence #8 - Third Point</u> - Write a sentence stating your third point. **(I also enjoy playing a musical instrument because it creates a lifelong enjoyment of music.)**

9. <u>Sentence #9 - Supporting Sentence(s)</u> - Write one or two sentences that give more information about your third point. **(Acquiring these special skills creates many opportunities for one to perform for business or pleasure throughout the rest of his or her life.)**

WRITING THE CONCLUSION

10. <u>Sentence #10 - Concluding General Statement</u> - Read the topic sentence again and then rewrite it, using some of the same words to say the same thing in a different way. **(Clearly, there are many advantages of playing a musical instrument.)**

11. <u>Sentence #11 - Concluding Summary (Final) Sentence</u> - Read the three-point sentence again and then rewrite it using some of the same words to say the same thing in a different way. **(For those who play a musical instrument, the skill can be very valuable in many ways.)**

SAMPLE THREE-PARAGRAPH ESSAY

The Benefits of Playing a Musical Instrument

I have discovered that playing a musical instrument can provide many opportunities for people who love music. Although many people focus solely on developing sports-related abilities, I think musical talents are just as important to develop. Playing a musical instrument opens the door to a new world of art, teaches self-discipline, and creates a lifelong enjoyment of music.

One of the reasons I enjoy playing a musical instrument is that it opens the door to a new world of art. In learning to play different pieces of music on an instrument, one explores a wide range of artistic styles. Another reason I enjoy playing a musical instrument is that it teaches self-discipline. Without a doubt, it requires devotion to the instrument. I also enjoy playing a musical instrument because it creates a lifelong enjoyment of music. Acquiring these special skills creates many opportunities for one to perform for business or pleasure throughout the rest of his or her life.

Clearly, there are many advantages of playing a musical instrument. For those who play a musical instrument, the skill can be very valuable in many ways.

Reference 31: Capitalization Rules

SECTION 1: CAPITALIZE THE FIRST WORD

1. The first word of a sentence. (*He likes to take a nap.*)
2. The first word in the greeting and closing of letters. (*Dear, Yours truly*)
3. The first and last word and important words in titles of literary works.
   (*books, songs, short stories, poems, articles, movie titles, magazines*)
   (*Note: Conjunctions, articles, and prepositions with fewer than five letters are not capitalized unless they are the first or last word.*)
4. The first word of a direct quotation. (*Dad said, "We are going home."*)
5. The first word in each line of a topic outline.

SECTION 2: CAPITALIZE NAMES, INITIALS, AND TITLES OF PEOPLE

6. The pronoun I. (*May I go with you?*)
7. The names and nicknames of people. (*Sam, Joe, Jones, Slim, Shorty*)
8. Family names when used in place of or with the person's name.
   (*Grandmother, Auntie, Uncle Joe, Mother – Do NOT capitalize <u>my mother</u>.*)
9. Titles used with, or in place of, people's names.
   (*Mr., Ms., Miss, Dr. Smith, Doctor, Captain, President, Sir*)
10. People's initials. (*J. D., C. Smith*)

SECTION 3: CAPITALIZE WORDS OF TIME

11. The days of the week and months of the year. (*Monday, July*)
12. The names of holidays. (*Christmas, Thanksgiving, Easter*)
13. The names of historical events, periods, laws, documents, conflicts, and distinguished awards. (*Civil War, Middle Ages, Medal of Honor*)

SECTION 4: CAPITALIZE NAMES OF PLACES

14. The names and abbreviations of cities, towns, counties, states, countries, and nations.
    (*Dallas, Texas, Fulton County, Africa, America, USA, AR, TX*)
15. The names of avenues, streets, roads, highways, routes, and post office boxes.
    (*Main Street, Jones Road, Highway 89, Rt. 1, Box 2, P.O. Box 45*)
16. The names of lakes, rivers, oceans, mountain ranges, deserts, parks, stars, planets, and constellations. (*Beaver Lake, Rocky Mountains, Venus*)
17. The names of schools and titles of school courses that are numbered or are languages.
    (*Walker Elementary School, Mathematics II*)
18. North, south, east, and west when they refer to sections of the country.
    (*up North, live in the East, out West*)

SECTION 5: CAPITALIZE NAMES OF OTHER NOUNS AND PROPER ADJECTIVES

19. The names of pets. (*Spot, Tweety Bird, etc.*)
20. The names of products. (*Campbell's soup, Kelly's chili, Ford cars, etc.*)
21. The names of companies, buildings, ships, planes, space ships.
    (*Empire State Building, Titanic, IBM, The Big Tire Co.*)
22. Proper adjectives. (*the English language, Italian restaurant, French test*)
23. The names of clubs, organizations, or groups. (*Lion's Club, Jaycees, Beatles*)
24. The names of political parties, religious preferences, nationalities, and races.
    (*Democratic party, Republican, Jewish synagogue, American*)

Reference 32: Sentence Parts That Can Be Used for a Pattern 1 Sentence

1. **Nouns**
   Use only subject nouns or object of the preposition nouns.

2. **Adverbs**
   Tell how, when, or where.
   Can be placed before or after verbs, at the beginning or end of a sentence, and in front of adjectives or other adverbs.

3. **Adjectives**
   Tell what kind, which one, or how many.
   Can be placed in front of nouns. Sometimes two or three adjectives can modify the same noun.

   Articles
   Adjectives that are used in front of nouns (a, an, the).

4. **Verbs** *(Can include helping verbs.)*

5. **Prepositional Phrases**
   Can be placed before or after nouns, after verbs, adverbs, or other prepositional phrases, and at the beginning or end of a sentence.

6. **Pronouns**
   (subjective, possessive, or objective)

7. **Conjunctions**
   Connecting words for compound parts: and, or, but.

8. **Interjections**
   Usually found at the beginning of a sentence. Can show strong or mild emotion.

Reference 33A: Punctuation Rules

SECTION 1: END MARK PUNCTUATION

1. Use a (.) for the end punctuation of a sentence that makes a statement.
   (*Mom baked us a cake.*)
2. Use a (?) for the end punctuation of a sentence that asks a question.
   (*Are you going to town?*)
3. Use an (!) for the end punctuation of a sentence that expresses strong feeling.
   (*That bee stung me!*)
4. Use a (.) for the end punctuation of a sentence that gives a command or makes a request.
   (*Close the door.*)

SECTION 2: COMMAS TO SEPARATE TIME WORDS

5. Use a comma between the day of the week and the month. (*Friday, July 23*)
   Use a comma between the day and year. (*July 23, 2009*)
6. Use a comma to separate the year from the rest of the sentence when the year follows the month or the month and the day.
   (*We spent May, 2001, with Mom. We spent July 23, 2001, with Dad.*)

SECTION 3: COMMAS TO SEPARATE PLACE WORDS

7. Use a comma to separate the city from the state or country.
   (*I will go to Dallas, Texas. He is from Paris, France.*)
8. Use a comma to separate the state or country from the rest of the sentence when the name of the state or country follows the name of a city.
   (*We flew to Dallas, Texas, in June. We flew to Paris, France, in July.*)

SECTION 4: COMMAS TO MAKE MEANINGS CLEAR

9. Use a comma to separate words or phrases in a series.
   (*We had soup, crackers, and milk.*)
10. Use commas to separate introductory words such as *Yes, Well, Oh,* and *No* from the rest of a sentence.
    (*Oh, I didn't know that.*)
11. Use commas to set off most appositives. An appositive is a word, phrase, title, or degree used directly after another word or name to explain it or to rename it.
    (*Sue, the girl next door, likes to draw.*)
    One-word appositives can be written two different ways: *(1) My brother, Tim, is riding in the horse show. (2) My brother Tim is riding in the horse show. (Your assignments will require one-word appositives to be set off with commas.)*
12. Use commas to separate a noun of direct address (the name of a person directly spoken to) from the rest of the sentence.
    (*Mom, do I really have to go?*)

SECTION 5: PUNCTUATION IN GREETINGS AND CLOSINGS OF LETTERS

13. Use a comma (,) after the salutation (greeting) of a friendly letter. (*Dear Sam,*)
14. Use a comma (,) after the closing of any letter. (*Yours truly,*)
15. Use a colon (:) after the salutation (greeting) of a business letter. (*Dear Madam:*)

Reference 33B: Punctuation Rules

SECTION 6: PERIODS

16. Use a period after most abbreviations or titles that are accepted in formal writing.
    (*Mr., Ms., Dr., Capt., St., Ave., St. Louis*) (*Note: These abbreviations cannot be used by themselves. They must always be used with a proper noun.*)

    In the abbreviations of many well-known organizations or words, periods are not required. (*USA, GM, TWA, GTE, AT&T, TV, AM, FM, GI, etc.*) Use only one period after an abbreviation at the end of a statement. Do not put an extra period for the end mark punctuation.

17. Use a period after initials.
    (*C. Smith, D.J. Brewton, Thomas A. Jones*)

18. Place a period after Roman numerals, Arabic numbers, and letters of the alphabet in an outline.
    (*II., IV., 5., 25., A., B.*)

SECTION 7: APOSTROPHES

19. Form a contraction by using an apostrophe in place of a letter or letters that have been left out.
    (*I'll, he's, isn't, wasn't, can't*)

20. Form the possessive of singular and plural nouns by using an apostrophe.
    (*boy's baseball, boys' baseball, children's baseball*)

21. Form the plurals of letters, symbols, numbers, and signs with the apostrophe plus *s* (*'s*).
    (*9's, B's, b's*)

SECTION 8: UNDERLINING

22. Use underlining or italics for titles of books, magazines, works of art, ships, newspapers, motion pictures, etc. (*A famous movie is <u>Gone With the Wind</u>. Our newspaper is the <u>Cabot Star Herald</u>.*) (*<u>Titanic</u>, <u>Charlotte's Web</u>, etc.*)

SECTION 9: QUOTATION MARKS

23. Use quotation marks to set off the titles of songs, short stories, short poems, articles, essays, short plays, and book chapters.
    (*Do you like to sing the song "America" in music class?*)

24. Quotation marks are used at the beginning and end of the person's words to separate what the person actually said from the rest of the sentence. Since the quotation tells what is being said, it will always have quotation marks around it.

25. The words that tell who is speaking are the explanatory words. Do not set explanatory words off with quotation marks. (*Fred said, "I'm here."*) (**Fred said** *are explanatory words and should not be set off with quotations.*)

26. A new paragraph is used to indicate a change of speaker.

27. When a speaker's speech is longer than one paragraph, quotation marks are used at the beginning of each paragraph and at the end of the last paragraph of that speaker's speech.

28. Use single quotation marks to enclose a quotation within a quotation.
    "My teddy bear says 'I love you' four different ways," said little Amy.

29. Use a period at the end of explanatory words that come at the end of a sentence.

30. Use a comma to separate a direct quotation from the explanatory words.

Reference 34: Capitalization and Punctuation Examples

```
    1   6                        9   7                    14   14
1. No, I didn't see the pictures Mr. Jones took of his vacation in Paris, France.
   10  19                       16                             8      1
```

Editing Guide for Sentence 1: Capitals: 6   Periods: 1   Commas: 2   Apostrophes: 1   End Marks: 1

```
      Y    D                        R
2. yes, david, my brother's pen pal, is russian.
```

Editing Guide for Sentence 2:   Capitals: 3   Commas: 3   Apostrophes: 1   End Marks: 1

Reference 35: Three-Paragraph Essay and Five-Paragraph Essay

Outline of a 3-Paragraph Essay	Outline of a 5-Paragraph Essay
I. Title	I. Title
II. Paragraph 1 – Introduction (3 sentences) A. Topic and general number sentence B. Extra information about the topic sentence C. Three-point sentence	II. Paragraph 1 – Introduction (3 sentences) A. Topic and general number sentence B. Extra information about the topic sentence C. Three-point sentence
III. Paragraph 2 – Body (6-9 sentences) A. **First-point** sentence B. One or two **supporting** sentences for the first point C. **Second-point** sentence D. One or two **supporting** sentences for the second point E. **Third-point** sentence F. One or two **supporting** sentences for the third point	III. Paragraph 2 - First Point Body (3-4 sentences) A. **First-point** sentence B. Two or three **supporting** sentences for the first point
	IV. Paragraph 3 – Second Point Body (3-4 sentences) A. **Second-point** sentence B. Two or three **supporting** sentences for the second point
IV. Paragraph 3 – Conclusion (2 sentences) A. Concluding general statement B. Concluding summary sentence	V. Paragraph 4 – Third Point Body (3-4 sentences) A. **Third-point** sentence B. Two or three **supporting** sentences for the third point
	VI. Paragraph 5 – Conclusion (2 sentences) A. Concluding general statement (Restatement of the topic sentence) B. Concluding summary sentence (Restatement of the 3-point sentence)

Reference 36: Steps in Writing a Five-Paragraph Expository Essay

WRITING TOPIC: Playing a Musical Instrument

THREE MAIN POINTS

♦ Select the points to list about the topic.

1. **Opens the door to a new world of art**
2. **Teaches self-discipline**
3. **Creates lifelong enjoyment of music**

WRITING THE INTRODUCTION AND TITLE

1. Sentence #1 - Topic Sentence
   Write the topic sentence by using the words in your topic and adding a general number word, such as *several, many, some,* or *numerous,* instead of the exact number of points you will discuss. **(I have discovered that playing a musical instrument can provide many opportunities for people who love music.)**

2. Sentence #2 - Extra Information about the topic sentence
   This sentence can clarify, explain, define, or just be an extra interesting comment about the topic sentence. If you need another sentence to complete your information, write an extra sentence here. If you write an extra sentence, your introductory paragraph will have four sentences in it instead of three and that is okay. **(Although many people focus solely on developing sports-related abilities, I think musical talents are just as important to develop.)**

3. Sentence #3 - Three-point sentence
   This sentence will list the three points to be discussed in the order that you will present them in the body of your paper. You can list the points with or without the specific number in front. **(Playing a musical instrument opens the door to a new world of art, teaches self-discipline, and creates a lifelong enjoyment of music.)** or **(The three reasons why I enjoy playing a musical instrument are that it opens the door to a new world of art, teaches self-discipline, and creates a lifelong enjoyment of music.)**

♦ The Title - Since there are many possibilities for titles, look at the topic and the three points listed about the topic. Use some of the words in the topic and write a phrase to tell what your paragraph is about. Your title can be short or long. Capitalize the first, last, and important words in your title. **(The Benefits of Playing a Musical Instrument)**

WRITING THE BODY

4. Sentence #4 - First Point - Write a sentence stating your first point. **(One of the reasons I enjoy playing a musical instrument is that it opens the door to a new world of art.)**

5. Sentences #5 - #7 - Supporting Sentences - Write two or three sentences that give more information about your first point. **(In learning to play different pieces of music on an instrument, one explores a wide range of artistic styles.) (In his or her career, a musician is able to explore numerous musical compositions.) (This exploration allows the musician to develop a taste for a variety of styles.)**

6. Sentence #8 - Second Point - Write a sentence stating your second point. **(Another reason I enjoy playing a musical instrument is that it teaches self-discipline.)**

7. Sentences #9 - #11 - Supporting Sentences - Write two or three sentences that give more information about your second point. **(Without a doubt, it requires devotion to the instrument.) (Many of the skills it takes to play well are acquired only through practice and patience.) (Often a musician must allow for extra hours of practice.)**

Reference 36: Steps in Writing a Five-Paragraph Expository Essay (continued)

8. Sentence #12 - Third Point - Write a sentence stating your third point.
   (I also enjoy playing a musical instrument because it creates a lifelong enjoyment of music.)

9. Sentences #13 - #15 - Supporting Sentences - Write two or three sentences that give more information about your third point.
   (Acquiring these special skills creates many opportunities for one to perform for business or pleasure throughout the rest of his or her life.) (A musician can perform in an orchestra, ensemble, or just play solo.) (Whether his or her audience is a crowded auditorium or just Mom and Dad, the overwhelming feeling of achievement and enjoyment is astounding.)

WRITING THE CONCLUSION

10. Sentence #16 - Concluding General Statement - Read the topic sentence again and then rewrite it, using some of the same words to say the same thing in a different way.
    (Clearly, there are many advantages of playing a musical instrument.)

11. Sentence #17 - Concluding Summary (final) Sentence - Read the three-point sentence again and then rewrite it, using some of the same words to say the same thing in a different way.
    (For those who play a musical instrument, the skill can be very valuable in many ways.)

SAMPLE FIVE-PARAGRAPH ESSAY

The Benefits of Playing a Musical Instrument

I have discovered that playing a musical instrument can provide many opportunities for people who love music. Although many people focus solely on developing sports-related abilities, I think musical talents are just as important to develop. Playing a musical instrument opens the door to a new world of art, teaches self-discipline, and creates a lifelong enjoyment of music.

One of the reasons I enjoy playing a musical instrument is that it opens the door to a new world of art. In learning to play different pieces of music on an instrument, one explores a wide range of artistic styles. In his or her career, a musician is able to explore numerous musical compositions. This exploration allows the musician to develop a taste for a variety of styles.

Another reason I enjoy playing a musical instrument is that it teaches self-discipline. Without a doubt, it requires devotion to the instrument. Many of the skills it takes to play well are acquired only through practice and patience. Often a musician must allow for extra hours of practice.

I also enjoy playing a musical instrument because it creates a lifelong enjoyment of music. Acquiring these special skills creates many opportunities for one to perform for business or pleasure throughout the rest of his or her life. A musician can perform in an orchestra, ensemble, or just play solo. Whether his or her audience is a crowded auditorium or just Mom and Dad, the overwhelming feeling of achievement and enjoyment is astounding.

Clearly, there are many advantages of playing a musical instrument. For those who play a musical instrument, the skill can be very valuable in many ways.

Reference 37: Persuasive Paragraph and Essay Guidelines

Guidelines for a Persuasive Paragraph

Paragraph   (10-13 sentences)

A. **Topic** sentence (opinion statement)
B. **General number** sentence
C. **First-point** persuasive sentence
D. 1 or 2 **supporting** sentences
 for the first point
E. **Second-point** persuasive sentence
F. 1 or 2 **supporting** sentences
 for the second point
G. **Third-point** persuasive sentence
H. 1 or 2 **supporting** sentences
 for the third point
I. **In conclusion** sentence
 (Repeat topic idea)
J. **Final summary** sentence
 (Summarize reasons)

Guidelines for a 3-Paragraph Persuasive Essay

I. Paragraph 1 – Introduction   (3 sentences)
  A. **Topic** sentence (opinion statement)
  B. **Reason** sentence
  C. **General number** sentence

II. Paragraph 2 – Body   (6-9 sentences)
  A. **First-point** persuasive sentence
  B. 1 or 2 **supporting** sentences for the first point
  C. **Second-point** persuasive sentence
  D. 1 or 2 **supporting** sentences for the second point
  E. **Third-point** persuasive sentence
  F. 1 or 2 **supporting** sentences for the third point

III. Paragraph 3 – Conclusion   (2 sentences)
  A. **In conclusion** sentence *(Repeat topic idea)*
  B. **Final summary** sentence *(Summarize reasons)*

Hats

Everyone should wear a hat with his or her outfit. Hats are the most exciting part of an outfit. There are numerous reasons why wearing a hat is beneficial.

The first benefit of wearing a hat is protection from the sun. Hats shield your head and face from harmful rays that can cause painful sunburns. The second benefit for wearing a hat is that hats provide a simple form of self-expression. Different styles of hats show others a lot about you. The third benefit of wearing a hat is that hats are not only fun, but also very versatile. You can find hats to match any outfit, style, or occasion.

In conclusion, every outfit should have a coordinating hat. By providing protection and fun, hats become a necessity for every outfit.

Reference 38: Direct Object, Verb-transitive, and Pattern 2

1. A **direct object** is a noun or pronoun after the verb that completes the meaning of the sentence.

2. A **direct object** is labeled as **DO**.

3. To find the **direct object**, ask WHAT or WHOM after the verb.

4. A **direct object** must be verified to mean someone or something different from the subject noun.

5. A **verb-transitive** is an action verb with a direct object after it and is labeled V-t. (Whatever receives the action of a transitive verb is the direct object.)

Sample Sentence for the exact words to say to find the direct object and transitive verb.

1. Bob wrote a novel.

2. Who wrote a novel? Bob - SN

3. What is being said about Bob? Bob wrote - V

4. Bob wrote what? novel - verify the noun

5. Does novel mean the same thing as Bob? No.

6. Novel - DO *(Say: Novel - direct object.)*

7. Wrote - V-t *(Say: Wrote - verb-transitive.)*

8. A - A

9. SN V-t DO P2 Check

   (Say: Subject Noun, Verb-transitive, Direct Object, Pattern 2, Check. This first check is to make sure the "t" is added to the verb.)

10. Verb-transitive - check again.

    ("Check again" means to check for prepositional phrases and then go through the rest of the Question and Answer Flow.)

11. No prepositional phrases.

12. Period, statement, declarative sentence

13. Go back to the verb - divide the complete subject from the complete predicate.

Reference 39: Regular Editing Checklist

Read each sentence and go through the Sentence Checkpoints below.

_____   E1. Sentence sense check. (Check for words left out or words repeated.)

_____   E2. First word, capital letter check. End mark check. Any other capitalization check. Any other punctuation check.

_____   E3. Sentence structure and punctuation check.
(Check for correct construction and correct punctuation of a simple sentence, a simple sentence with compound parts, or a compound sentence.)

_____   E4. Spelling and homonym check.
(Check for misspelled words and incorrect homonym choices.)

_____   E5. Usage check.
(Check subject-verb agreement, a/an choice, pronoun/antecedent agreement, pronoun cases, degrees of adjectives, double negatives, verb tenses, and contractions.)

Read each paragraph and go through the Paragraph Checkpoints below.

_____   E6. Check to see that each paragraph is indented.

_____   E7. Check each paragraph for a topic sentence.

_____   E8. Check each sentence to make sure it supports the topic of the paragraph.

_____   E9. Check the content for interest and creativity. Do not begin all sentences with the same word, and use a variety of simple, compound, and complex sentences.

_____   E10. Check the type and format of the writing assigned.

Reference 40: Editing Example

Topic: **Reasons police officers use German shepherds**
Three main points: **(1. size   2. keen sense of smell   3. intelligence)**

Officers

German Shepherds for Police officers

→   U   S   G   (.) A
Police officers all over the united states use german shepherds for several reasons although German

often   a
shepherds are oftan companion dogs, it is the police officer that has made the German shepherd an popular

reasons   their   their
working dog. Three reason police officers use German shepherds are its size, its keen sense of smell, and

their   (.)
 its intelligence

their
    The first reason that police officers use German shepherds is there size. The strong, sleek body of

G   shepherd
the german shepard is very intimidating to anyone who is a threat to police officers. The second reason that police

their   (,)   many   (,)
officers use German shepherds is there keen sense of smell. German shepherds like miny other dogs can

noses   scents
use their nose's to follow cents left by criminals that humans would not be able to follow. The third reason

their
that police officers use German shepherds is its intelligence. Because German shepherds are a very smart

they're   obey   (.)
breed of dog, their easily trained to readily obeys the commands of their officer

reasons   (')   (,)
    In conclusion, police officers use German shepherds for many reason. The German shepherds size

(,)   make   police   (.)
keen sense of smell and intelligence makes them valuable working companions to the poliece officer

Total Mistakes: 34
Editing Guide: Sentence checkpoints: **E1, E2, E3, E4, E5**   Paragraph checkpoints: **E6, E7, E8, E9, E10**

Reference 41: Complete Sentences and Sentence Fragments

PART 1: Identifying Sentences and Fragments

Identifying simple sentences and fragments: Write **S** for a complete sentence and **F** for a sentence fragment on the line beside each group of words below.

S	1. The river flowed swiftly.
F	2. In their tracks.
S	3. Trumpets blared.
F	4. Crawling across the ceiling.
F	5. The enormous boulder.

PART 2: Sentence Fragments

Fragment Examples: (1) prepared to jump (2) all the happy children (3) because I snore too loudly
(4) Washing the car.

Reference 41: Complete Sentences and Sentence Fragments (continued)

PART 3: Correcting Sentence Fragments

Directions: Add the part that is underlined in parentheses to make each fragment into a complete sentence.

1. In the cave during the winter months.
   (subject part, predicate part, <u>both the subject and predicate</u>)
   (**The grizzly bear slept soundly** in the cave during the winter months.)

2. The chocolate milk.
   (subject part, <u>predicate part</u>, both the subject and predicate)
   (The chocolate milk **spilled on my dress**.)

3. Galloped excitedly by the creek during the storm.
   (<u>subject part</u>, predicate part, both the subject and predicate)
   (**The horses** galloped excitedly by the creek during the storm.)

Reference 42: Simple Sentences, Compound Parts, and Fragments

Example 1: The red car rolled slowly down the hill. (**S**)

Example 2: <u>Stacy and Bonnie</u> worked at the bank. (**SCS**)

Example 3: Kim <u>painted and decorated</u> her bedroom. (**SCV**)

Part 1: Identify each kind of sentence by writing the abbreviation in the blank. (**S, SS, F, SCS, SCV**)

SCV 1. The students sang and danced in the play.

SCS 2. The horse and buggy arrived today.

F 3. After the trip to the zoo.

S 4. The ducks flew south for the winter.

SS 5. I turned on the air conditioner. It cooled the hot room.

Part 2: Put a slash to separate each run-on sentence below. Then, correct the run-on sentences by rewriting them as indicated by the labels in parentheses at the end of each sentence.

1. The young girl was crying **/** she was lost. (**SS**)
   The young girl was crying. She was lost.

2. The trophy is in the glass case **/** the medal is in the glass case. (**SCS**)
   The trophy and medal are in the glass case.

3. The toddler splashed in the water **/** she played in the water for hours. (**SCV**)
   The toddler splashed and played in the water for hours.

Reference 43: The Compound Sentence

1. Compound means two. A compound sentence is two complete sentences joined together correctly. The abbreviation for a compound sentence is **CD**.

2. <u>One way to join two sentences</u> and make a compound sentence is to <u>use a comma and a conjunction</u>. The formula for you to follow will always be given at the end of the sentence. The formula gives the abbreviation for the compound sentence and lists the conjunction to use (**CD, and**). Remember to place the comma BEFORE the conjunction.

   Example 1: We saw deer tracks in the **woods, and** we followed them. (CD, and)

3. <u>Another way to join two sentences</u> and make a compound sentence is to <u>use a semicolon only</u>. The formula to follow is given at the end of the sentence and lists the semicolon after the abbreviation of the compound sentence (**CD;**). (This method is usually used with short sentences that are closely related in thought.)

   Example 2: We saw deer tracks in the **woods; we** followed them. (CD;)

4. Compound sentences should be closely related in thought and importance.

   Correct: We saw deer tracks in the **woods, and** we followed them.
   Incorrect: We saw deer tracks in the **woods, and** my sister went shopping
   at the mall.

Reference 44: Ways to Correct Compound Sentence Mistakes

When a compound sentence is not joined together correctly, you have a **comma splice or a run-on sentence.**

1. **A comma splice** is two sentences incorrectly connected with a comma and no conjunction. To correct a comma splice: Put a conjunction (*and, or, but*) after the comma.

   Incorrect: I love **horses, I** ride every day.
   Correct: I love **horses, and I** ride every day.

2. **A run-on sentence** is two or more sentences written together as one sentence, or two or more sentences written with a conjunction and no comma.

   Incorrect: I love **horses I** ride every day.
   Incorrect: I love **horses and I** ride every day.

3. Below are two ways to correct a run-on sentence:

   1. Put a comma and a conjunction between the two complete thoughts.
   2. Put a semicolon between the two complete thoughts.

   Correct: I love **horses, and I** ride every day.
   Correct: I love **horses; I** ride every day.

Reference 45: Using SCS, SCV, and CD Correctly

Put a slash to separate the two complete thoughts in each run-on sentence. Correct the run-on sentences or fragments as indicated by the labels in parentheses at the end of each sentence.

1. Samantha loves the state fair **/** she doesn't like the scary rides. (**CD**, but)
   Samantha loves the state fair, but she doesn't like the scary rides.

2. My dad owns a famous restaurant **/** the food is delicious! (**CD**;)
   My dad owns a famous restaurant; the food is delicious!

3. Beth sings in the church choir **/** Mary sings in the church choir. (**SCS**)
   Beth and Mary sing in the church choir. *(When the subject is compound, the verb is plural.)*

4. For extra money, David mows lawns **/** he cleans garages. (**SCV**)
   For extra money, David mows lawns and cleans garages.

Reference 46: Identifying S, F, SCS, SCV, CD

Part 1: Identify each kind of sentence by writing the abbreviation in the blank. (**S, F, SCS, SCV, CD**)

   CD   1. Mr. Samson wanted to read the report; but he forgot his glasses.

   S   2. Dr. Robertson teaches first aid to the students at the high school.

   CD   3. We played tag at recess, but we did not play ball.

   SCS   4. Scott and Jerry rode the bus to the park.

   F   5. In the winter, the strong cold wind.

   SCV   6. My father climbed the tree and pulled my kite from the branches.

Part 2: On notebook paper, use the ways listed below to correct this run-on sentence:

I baked a cake I did not eat it.

7. CD, but   **I baked a cake, but I did not eat it.**   8. SCV   **I baked a cake but did not eat it.**

Reference 47: Personal Pronoun-Antecedent Agreement

                    antecedent   pronoun   antecedent   pronoun
A. The little *boy* grinned playfully at *his* brother. **B.** The little *boy* gasped. *He* had just been stung.

1. Decide if the antecedent is singular or plural, and then choose the pronoun that agrees in number.

   If the antecedent is singular, the pronoun must be singular. (man - he, him, his, etc.)
   If the antecedent is plural, the pronoun must be plural. (men - they, them, their, etc.)

2. Decide if the antecedent is male or female, and then choose the pronoun that agrees in gender.

   If the antecedent is masculine, the pronoun must be masculine gender. (boy-he)
   If the antecedent is feminine, the pronoun must be feminine gender. (girl-she)
   If the antecedent is neither masculine nor feminine, the pronoun must be the neuter gender. (book, it)

(The plural pronouns *they* and *them* also show the neuter gender. The **toys** are damaged. **They** are broken.)

Guided Practice for Antecedent Agreement

Choose an answer from the pronoun choices in parentheses. Then, fill in the rest of the columns according to the titles. (**S** or **P** stands for singular or plural.)

Pronoun-Antecedent Agreement	Pronoun choice	S or P	Antecedent	S or P
1. The princess was proud of (<u>her</u>, their) crown.	her	S	princess	S
2. The doctor finally revealed (<u>his</u>, their) age.	his	S	doctor	S
3. The pheasants laid (its, <u>their</u>) eggs in the grass.	their	P	pheasants	P

Reference 48: Making Nouns Possessive

1. For a singular noun - add (**'s**)	2. For a plural noun that ends in **s** - add (**'**)	3. For a plural noun that does not end in **s** - add (**'s**)
Rule 1: girl's	**Rule 2: girls'**	**Rule 3: women's**

Part A: Underline each noun to be made possessive and write singular or plural (**S-P**), the rule number, and the possessive form. Part B: Write each noun as singular possessive and then as plural possessive.

Part A	S-P	Rule	Possessive Form	Part B	Singular Poss	Plural Poss
1. <u>magician</u> cape	S	1	magician's cape	5. knife	knife's	knives'
2. <u>nurses</u> patients	P	2	nurses' patients	6. broom	broom's	brooms'
3. <u>James</u> mailbox	S	1	James's mailbox	7. inventor	inventor's	inventors'
4. <u>children</u> voices	P	3	children's voices	8. man	man's	men's

Reference 49: Indirect Object and Pattern 3

1. An **indirect object** is a noun or pronoun.

2. An **indirect object** receives what the direct object names.

3. An **indirect object** is located between the verb-transitive and the direct object.

4. An **indirect object** is labeled as **IO**.

5. To find the **indirect object**, ask TO WHOM or FOR WHOM after the direct object.

Sample Sentence for the exact words to say to find the indirect object.

1. Mother baked me a cake.
2. Who baked me a cake? Mother - SN
3. What is being said about Mother? Mother baked - V
4. Mother baked what? cake - verify the noun
5. Does cake mean the same thing as Mother? No.
6. Cake - DO
7. Baked - V-t
8. Mother baked cake for whom? me - IO
   (Say: Me - indirect object.)
9. A - A

10. SN V-t IO DO P3 Check
    (Say: Subject Noun, Verb-transitive, Indirect Object, Direct Object, Pattern 3, Check.) (This first check is to make sure the "t" is added to the verb.)
11. Verb-transitive - check again.
    ("Check again" means to check for prepositional phrases and then go through the rest of the Question and Answer Flow.)
12. No prepositional phrases.
13. Period, statement, declarative sentence.
14. Go back to the verb - divide the complete subject from the complete predicate.

Reference 50: Quotation Rules for Beginning Quotes

1. **Pattern:** "C -quote- (,!?) " <u>explanatory words</u> (.)
   (Quotation marks, capital letter, quote, end punctuation choice, quotation marks closed, explanatory words, period)

2. Underline **end explanatory words** and use a period at the end.

3. You should have a **beginning quote** – Use quotation marks at the beginning and end of what is said. Then, put a comma, question mark, or exclamation point (no period) after the quote but in front of the quotation marks.

4. **Capitalize** the beginning of the quote, any proper nouns, or the pronoun *I*.

5. **Punctuate** the rest of the sentence by checking for any apostrophes, periods, or commas that may be needed within the sentence.

Guided Practice

Sentence: the girls and i are writing invitations next monday with mrs kemp andy said

1. Pattern: "C -quote- (,!?) " <u>explanatory words</u> (.)

2. the girls and i are writing invitations next monday with mrs kemp <u>**andy said**</u>(.)

3. "the girls and i are writing invitations next monday with mrs kemp**,"** <u>andy said</u>.

4. "**The** girls and **I** are writing invitations next **M**onday with **Mrs K**emp," <u>**A**ndy said</u>.

5. "The girls and I are writing invitations next Monday with Mrs. Kemp," <u>Andy said</u>.

6. **Corrected Sentence:** "The girls and I are writing invitations next Monday with Mrs. Kemp," Andy said.

Reference 51: Quotation Rules for End Quotes

1. **Pattern:** C - explanatory words(,) "C -quote- (.!?) "
   (Capital letter, explanatory words, comma, quotation marks, capital letter, quote, end punctuation choice, quotation marks closed)

2. Underline **beginning explanatory words** and use a comma after them.

3. You should have an **end quote** – Use quotation marks at the beginning and end of what is said. Then, put a period, question mark, or exclamation point (no comma) after the quote, but in front of the quotation marks.

4. **Capitalize** the first of the explanatory words at the beginning of a sentence, the beginning of the quote, and any proper nouns or the pronoun *I*.

5. **Punctuate** the rest of the sentence by checking for any apostrophes, periods, or commas that may be needed within the sentence.

Guided Practice

Sentence: andy said the girls and i are writing invitations next monday with mrs kemp

1. Pattern: C - explanatory words(,) "C - quote- (.!?) "

2. <u>**andy said**</u>(,) the girls and i are writing invitations next monday with mrs kemp

3. <u>andy said</u>, "the girls and i are writing invitations next monday with mrs kemp**. "**

4. <u>Andy said</u>, "**T**he girls and **I** are writing invitations next **M**onday with **M**rs **K**emp."

5. <u>Andy said</u>, "The girls and I are writing invitations next Monday with Mrs**.** Kemp."

6. **Corrected Sentence:** Andy said, "The girls and I are writing invitations next Monday with Mrs. Kemp."

Reference 52: Story Elements Outline

1. **Main Idea (Tell the problem or situation that needs a solution.)**
   Dillon's mother was gone, and he was worried and scared.

2. **Setting (Tell when and where the story takes place, either clearly stated or implied.)**
   When - The story takes place in the evening. Where - The story takes place at Dillon's house.

3. **Character (Tell whom or what the story is about.)**
   The main characters are Dillon and his dog.

4. **Plot (Tell what the characters in the story do and what happens to them.)**
   The story is about a boy's frightening experience while his mom goes to the store.

5. **Ending (Use a strong ending that will bring the story to a close.)**
   The story ends with Dillon's relief that the scary creature was his dog.

Dillon's Scare

Dillon sat quietly at the computer working on his history paper. His mom had gone to the store to get groceries for dinner that evening. It was getting late, and the sky began to darken outside. Dillon had stayed at home by himself many times, but his mom had been gone for a while now. He was getting worried.

"She'll be home anytime," he said to himself as he left the computer to look out the window one more time. With no sign of his mom's car, he headed back to his chair. Before he could sit down, there was a sound coming from the other room.

"Knock! Knock! Thump!" Dillon jumped and ran for the baseball bat he kept in the corner of his room. "Knock! Knock! Thump! Knock!" It sounded louder this time. Dillon slowly crept around the corner and into the other room. He glanced around the dark room and was about to leave when something in the far corner caught his attention. He flipped on the light switch.

"Molly! You silly dog!" Molly got up from scratching her fleas. She let out one big "Woof!" as she headed toward Dillon with her big paws thumping on the floor.

Reference 53: Regular and Irregular Verbs

Most verbs are **regular verbs**. This means that they form the past tense merely by adding **-ed**, **-d**, or **-t** to the main verb: *pace, paced*. This simple procedure makes regular verbs easy to identify. Some verbs, however, do not form their past tense in this way. For that reason, they are called **irregular verbs**. Most irregular verbs form the past tense by having a **vowel spelling change** in the word. For example: *drive, drove, driven* or *ring, rang, rung*.

To decide if a verb is regular or irregular, remember these two things:

1. Look only at the main verb. If the main verb is made past tense with an *-ed, -d, or -t* ending, it is a regular verb. (*pace, paced, paced*)

2. Look only at the main verb. If the main verb is made past tense with a vowel spelling change, it is an irregular verb. (*ring, rang, rung*)

A partial listing of the most common irregular verbs is on the irregular verb chart located in Reference 27 on page 23 in the student book. Refer to this chart whenever necessary.

Identify each verb as regular or irregular and put **R** or **I** in the blank. Then, write the past tense form.

ride	I	rode	sign	R	signed	eat	I	ate
try	R	tried	drive	I	drove	build	R	built

Reference 54: Simple Verb Tenses

When you are writing paragraphs, you must use verbs that are in the same tense. Tense means time. The tense of a verb shows the time of the action. There are three basic tenses that show when an action takes place. They are **present tense, past tense,** and **future tense**. These tenses are known as the simple tenses.

1. The **simple present tense** shows that something is happening now, in the present. The present tense form usually ends in *s, es,* or in a *plain ending*.

    (Regular present tense form: climb, climbs) (Irregular present tense form: ride, rides)
    (**Examples:** Jerry climbs a tall ladder. Carla rides wild horses.)

2. The **simple past tense** shows that something has happened sometime in the past. The regular past tense form usually ends in **-ed, -d, -t**. Most irregular past tense forms should be memorized.

    (Regular past tense form: *climbed*) (Irregular past tense form: *rode*)
    (**Examples:** Jerry climbed a tall ladder. Carla rode wild horses.)

3. The **future tense** shows that something will happen sometime in the future. The future tense form always has the helping verb *will* or *shall* before the main verb.

    (Regular future tense form: *will climb*) (Irregular future tense form: *will ride*)
    (**Examples:** Jerry will climb a tall ladder. Carla will ride wild horses.)

Simple Present Tense	Simple Past Tense	Simple Future Tense
What to look for: **one verb** With s, es, or plain ending.	What to look for: **one verb** With -ed, -d, -t, or irr spelling change.	What to look for: **will** or **shall** With a main verb.
1. He goes on a hike. 2. He does his homework.	1. He went on a hike. 2. He did his homework.	1. He will go on a hike. 2. He will do his homework.

Reference 55: Tenses of Helping Verbs

1. If there is only a main verb in a sentence, the tense is determined by the main verb and will be either present tense or past tense.

2. If there is a helping verb with a main verb, the tense of both verbs will be determined by the helping verb, not the main verb.

Since the helping verb determines a verb's tense, it is important to learn the tenses of the 14 helping verbs you will be using. You should memorize the list below so you will never have trouble with tenses.

Present tense helping verbs:	**am, is, are, has, have, does, do**
Past tense helping verbs:	**was, were, had, did, been**
Future tense helping verbs:	**will, shall**

If you use a present tense helping verb, it is considered present tense even though the main verb has an *-ed* ending and it doesn't sound like present tense. (*I have walked - present tense.*) In later grades, you will learn that certain helping verbs help form other tenses called the perfect tenses.

Example 1: Underline each verb or verb phrase. Identify the verb tense by writing a number **1** for present tense, a number **2** for past tense, or a number **3** for future tense. Write the past tense form and **R** or **I** for Regular or Irregular.

Verb Tense			Main Verb Past Tense Form	R or I
1		1. The bluebird <u>has built</u> a nest.	built	R
2		2. She <u>had written</u> her name in pencil.	wrote	I
3		3. The boys <u>will close</u> the gate.	closed	R

Example 2: List the present tense and past tense helping verbs below.

Present tense:	1. **am**	2. **is**	3. **are**	4. **has**	5. **have**	6. **does**	7. **do**
Past tense:	8. **was**	9. **were**	10. **had**	11. **did**	12. **been**		

Reference 56: Changing Tenses in Paragraphs

Guided Example 1: Change the underlined present tense verbs in Paragraph 1 to past tense verbs in Paragraph 2.

Paragraph 1: Present Tense

Lindsay **fills** her jar with lightening bugs every June. She **chases** them down hillsides and **grabs** them with her fingers. Once she **captures** them, she **drops** them into her see-through container, one at a time. She **prizes** them like jewels and **lets** them flash all night on the stand beside her bed.

Paragraph 2: Past Tense

Lindsay **filled** her jar with lightening bugs every June. She **chased** them down hillsides and **grabbed** them with her fingers. Once she **captured** them, she **dropped** them into her see-through container, one at a time. She **prized** them like jewels and **let** them flash all night on the stand beside her bed.

Guided Example 2: Change the underlined mixed tense verbs in Paragraph 1 to present tense verbs in Paragraph 2.

Paragraph 3: Mixed Tenses

My brother **went** fishing several times during the summer. He **throws** his line in the water and **caught** a fish almost every time. He **cleans** them and **grilled** them over an open fire. He usually **seasoned** them with Cajun spices. He **sat** under a shade tree in the evening breeze and **ate** them. Then, he **drifts** off to sleep.

Paragraph 4: Present Tense

My brother **goes** fishing several times during the summer. He **throws** his line in the water and **catches** a fish almost every time. He **cleans** them and **grills** them over an open fire. He usually **seasons** them with Cajun spices. He **sits** under a shade tree in the evening breeze and **eats** them. Then, he **drifts** off to sleep.

Reference 57: Double Negatives		
Negative Words That Begin With _N_	**Other Negative Words**	**Negative Prefixes**
neither no no one not (n't) nowhere never nobody none nothing	barely, hardly, scarcely	dis, non, un

Three Ways to Correct a Double Negative

Rule 1. **Change** the second negative to a positive:
       Wrong: The crowd **couldn't** see **nothing**.
       Right: The crowd **couldn't** see **anything**.

Rule 2. **Take out** the negative part of a contraction:
       Wrong: The crowd **couldn't** see **nothing**.
       Right: The crowd **could** see **nothing**.

Rule 3. **Remove** the first negative word (possibility of a verb change):
       Wrong: The crowd **couldn't** see **nothing**.
       Right: The crowd **saw nothing**.

Changing Negative Words to Positive Words

1. Change _no_ or _none_ to _any_.
2. Change _nobody_ to _anybody_.
3. Change _no one_ to _anyone_.
4. Change _nothing_ to _anything_.
5. Change _nowhere_ to _anywhere_.
6. Change _never_ to _ever_.
7. Change _neither_ to _either_.
8. Remove the _n't_ from a contraction.

Examples: Underline the negative words in each sentence. Rewrite each sentence and correct the double-negative mistake as indicated by the rule number in parentheses at the end of the sentence.

1. She <u>doesn't</u> have <u>no</u> money for lunch. (Rule 3) **She has no money for lunch.**

2. The seniors <u>can't</u> <u>hardly</u> wait for graduation. (Rule 2) **The seniors can hardly wait for graduation.**

3. He <u>hasn't</u> done <u>nothing</u> for his report. (Rule 1) **He hasn't done anything for his report.**

Reference 58: Contraction Chart				Pronoun	Contraction

AM
I am   – I'm

IS
is not   – isn't
he is   – he's
she is   – she's
it is   – it's
who is   – who's
that is   – that's
what is   – what's
there is   – there's

ARE
are not   – aren't
you are   – you're
we are   – we're
they are   – they're

WAS, WERE
was not   – wasn't
were not   – weren't

DO, DOES, DID
do not   – don't
does not   – doesn't
did not   – didn't

CAN
cannot   – can't

LET
let us   – let's

HAS
has not   – hasn't
he has   – he's
she has   – she's

HAVE
have not   – haven't
I have   – I've
you have   – you've
we have   – we've
they have   – they've

HAD
had not   – hadn't
I had   – I'd
he had   – he'd
she had   – she'd
you had   – you'd
we had   – we'd
they had   – they'd

WILL, SHALL
will not   – won't
I will   – I'll
he will   – he'll
she will   – she'll
you will   – you'll
we will   – we'll
they will   – they'll

WOULD
would not   – wouldn't
I would   – I'd
he would   – he'd
she would   – she'd
you would   – you'd
we would   – we'd
they would   – they'd

SHOULD, COULD
should not   – shouldn't
could not   – couldn't

Pronoun / Contraction

its
(owns)
its coat

it's
(it is)
it's cute

your
(owns)
your car

you're
(you are)
you're right

their
(owns)
their house

they're
(they are)
they're gone

whose
(owns)
whose cat

who's
(who is)
who's going

Reference 59: Linking Verbs

An action verb shows action. It tells what the subject does. A linking verb does not show action. It does not tell what the subject does. A linking verb is called a state of being verb because it tells **what the subject is or is like**. To decide if a verb is linking or action, remember these two things:

1. A linking verb may have a noun in the predicate that means the same thing as the subject:

A linking verb connects a noun in the predicate that means the same thing as the subject to the subject of the sentence. This noun is called a predicate noun and is identified with the abbreviation **PrN**.

(Mrs. Reid is the aunt.)   *(They are the players.)*   *(Kim is the friend.)*   *(Son is the actor.)*

    SN LV   PrN   SP LV   PrN   SN LV   PrN   SN LV   PrN
Mrs. Reid **is** my (aunt).   They **are** soccer (players).   Kim **is** my best (friend).   My son **is** a talented (actor).

2. A linking verb may also have an adjective in the predicate that tells what kind of subject:

A linking verb connects an adjective in the predicate that describes the subject of the sentence. This adjective is called a predicate adjective and is identified with the abbreviation **PA**.

(What kind of coach? happy) (What kind of Joe? hungry) (What kind of grass? green) (What kind of they? doubtful)

    SN LV PA   SN LV PA   SN LV PA   SP LV   PA
The coach **is** (happy).   Joe **was** (hungry).   The grass **is** (green).   They **were** very (doubtful).

These are the <u>most common</u> linking verbs: *am, is, are, was, were, be, been, seem, become.*
These <u>sensory verbs</u> can be linking or action: *taste, sound, smell, feel, look.*

A good rule to follow:
If a sentence has a predicate noun (**PrN**) or a predicate adjective (**PA**), it has a linking verb.
If a sentence <u>does not have</u> a predicate noun (**PrN**) or a predicate adjective (**PA**), it probably has an action verb.

Example: Underline each subject and fill in each column according to the title.

	List each Verb	Write PrN, PA, or None	Write L or A
1. The <u>clouds</u> are dark.	are	PA	L
2. The <u>choir</u> sings well.	sings	None	A
3. <u>Tony</u> is my first cousin.	is	PrN	L
4. The <u>squirrel</u> is climbing the tree.	is climbing	None	A

Reference 60: Rules for the Plurals of Nouns with Different Endings

1. "ch, sh, z, s, ss, x" – add "es."	6. "f" or "ff," add "s."
2. a vowel plus "y," add an "s."	7. a vowel plus "o," add "s."
3. a consonant plus "y," change "y" to "i" and add "es."	8. a consonant plus "o," add "es."
4. "f" or "fe," change the "f" or "fe" to "v" and add "es."	9. stays the same for S and P.
5. irregular nouns – change spellings completely.	10. regular nouns – add "s".

Use the rules above to write the correct plural form of these nouns:

	Rule	Plural Form			Rule	Plural Form
1. donkey	2	donkeys	3.	proof	6	proofs
2. elf	4	elves	4.	fish	9 or 1	fish or fishes

Reference 61: Guidelines for Descriptive Writing

1. **When describing people,** it is helpful to notice these types of details: appearance, walk, voice, manner, gestures, personality traits, any special incident related to the person being described, and any striking details that make that person stand out in your mind.

2. **When describing places or things,** it is helpful to notice these types of details: the physical features of a place or thing (color, texture, smell, shape, size, age), any unusual features, any special incident related to the place or thing being described, and whether or not the place or thing is special to you.

3. **When describing nature,** it is helpful to notice these types of details: the special features of the season, the sights, smells, sounds, colors, animals, insects, birds, and any special incident related to the scene being described.

4. **When describing an incident or an event,** it is helpful to notice these types of details: the order in which the event takes place, any specific facts that will keep the story moving from a beginning to an ending, the answers to any of the *who, what, when, where, why,* and *how* questions that the reader needs to know, and especially the details that will create a clear picture, such as how things look, sound, smell, feel, etc.

Reference 62: Descriptive Paragraph Guidelines

A. Sentence 1 is the topic sentence that introduces **what is being described**.

B. For sentences 2-8, use **the descriptive details** in Reference 61.

C. Sentence 9 is a concluding sentence that **restates, or relates back to, the topic sentence**.

A Weekend at the Cabin

Almost every weekend, my family and I pack our bags and drive to the lake for a weekend stay in our cabin. When we arrive, we spend the rest of the evening sitting by a small campfire near the edge of the lake. Dad unpacks his guitar and strums a few relaxing tunes. Mom dozes off in the hammock while Daniel and I comb the shoreline for unique treasures. We return to the cabin before dusk with a few old bobbers, a rusty can, and an empty glass bottle. We tromp up the front porch stairs and head inside to tell of our adventure. A little later, the family gathers in the front room to watch a movie. Daniel and I try to stay awake, but we soon fall fast asleep. Even though our trips to the cabin can be very tiresome, it is my favorite place to go on the weekend.

Reference 63: The Five Parts of a Friendly Letter

1. Heading

1. Box or street address of writer
2. City, state, zip code of writer
3. Date letter was written
4. Placement: upper right-hand corner

2. Friendly Greeting or Salutation

1. Begins with *Dear*
2. Names person receiving the letter
3. Has comma after person's name
4. Placement: at left margin, two lines below heading

3. Body

1. Tells reason the letter was written
2. Can have one or more paragraphs
3. Has indented paragraphs
4. Is placed one line below the greeting
5. Skips one line between each paragraph

4. Closing

1. Closes letter with a personal phrase (Your friend, With love,)
2. Capitalizes only first word
3. Is followed by a comma
4. Is placed two lines below the body
5. Begins just to the right of the middle of the letter

5. Signature

1. Tells who wrote the letter
2. Is usually signed in cursive
3. Uses first name only unless there is a question as to which friend or relative you are
4. Is placed beneath the closing

Reference 63: The Five Parts of a Friendly Letter (continued)

Friendly Letter Example

	1. Heading
	5481 Victory Blvd.
	Stocktown, WV 50009
	June 8, 20___

2.   Friendly Greeting, (or Salutation)
Dear Tim,

3.   Body (Indent Paragraphs)

As you know, your Uncle James and I will be going to Europe next month. We need someone to watch the house and take care of our dog. We thought you would be the perfect person for the job since you are on summer vacation. If you don't already have plans, we'd love for you to house-sit for us!

4. Closing,
Sincerely yours,

5. Signature
Aunt Tracey

Reference 64:   Envelope Parts

Envelope Parts	Friendly Envelope Example	
The return address:	**Return Address**	Stamp
1. Name of the person writing the letter	Tracey Graves	
2. Box or street address of the writer	5481 Victory Blvd.	
3. City, state, zip code of the writer	Stocktown, WV 50009	
The mailing address:	**Mailing Address**	
1. Name of the person receiving the letter	Tim Smith	
2. Street address of the person receiving the letter	123 Mockingbird Lane	
3. City, state, zip of the person receiving the letter	Jacksonville, FL 70006	

Reference 65: Four Types of Business Letters

Four common reasons to write business letters and information about the four types:

1. If you need to send for information - letter of inquiry.
2. If you want to order a product - letter of request or order.
3. If you want to express an opinion - letter to an editor or official.
4. If you want to complain about a product - letter of complaint.

Letter of Inquiry	Letter of Request or Order
1. Ask for information or answers to your questions. 2. Keep the letter short and to the point. 3. Word the letter so that there can be no question as to what it is you need to know.	1. Carefully and clearly describe the product. 2. Keep the letter short and to the point. 3. Include information on how and where the product should be shipped. 4. Include information on how you will pay for the product.
Letter to an Editor or Official	**Letter of Complaint About a Product**
1. Clearly explain the problem or situation. 2. Offer your opinion of the cause and possible solutions. 3. Support your opinions with facts and examples. 4. Suggest ways to change or improve the situation.	1. Carefully and clearly describe the product. 2. Describe the problem and what may have caused it. *(Don't spend too much time explaining how unhappy you are.)* 3. Explain any action you have already taken to solve the problem. 4. End your letter with the action you would like the company to take to solve the problem.

Reference 66: Business Letter Example

1. HEADING

47 Benton Road
Boise, Idaho 40007
March 30, 20__

2. INSIDE ADDRESS

Mr. Stanley Wolfe
Tucson Tickets and Travel
2737 Baxter Drive
Tucson, Arizona 20001

3. FORMAL GREETING, (OR SALUTATION)

Dear Mr. Wolfe:

4. BODY (INDENT PARAGRAPHS)

Our company is planning a semi-annual conference in June. We would like some information about the lodging and attractions that would be available to us. Any information you could send us would be much appreciated.

5. FORMAL CLOSING,

Sincerely yours,

6. SIGNATURE

Ken Jarvis

Reference 67: Business Envelope Parts

Envelope Parts	Business Envelope Example

The return address:
1. Name of the person writing the letter
2. Box or street address of the writer
3. City, state, zip code of the writer

The mailing address:
1. Name of the person receiving the letter
2. Name of the company receiving the letter
3. Street address of the person receiving the letter
4. City, state, zip of the person receiving the letter

Return Address   **Stamp**
Ken Jarvis
47 Benton Road
Boise, Idaho 40007

Mailing Address
Mr. Stanley Wolfe
Tucson Tickets and Travel
2737 Baxter Drive
Tucson, Arizona 20001

Reference 68: Thank-You Notes

	For a Gift		**For an Action**
What -	Thank you for... (tell color, kind, and item)	**What -**	Thank you for... (tell action)
Use -	Tell how the gift is used.	**Helped -**	Tell how the action helped.
Thanks -	I appreciate your remembering me with this special gift.	**Thanks -**	I appreciate your thinking of me at this time.

Example 1: Gift

202 Shady Lane
Gopher, Missouri 21161
January 12, 20___

Dear Lorene,

   The red scarf you sent me for Christmas is absolutely beautiful. I will always think of you as I wear it this winter. I appreciate this special gift that you made especially for me.

Much love,
Aunt Ellen

Example 2: Action

420 Elmwood Place
Harpoon, Louisiana 47705
June 26, 20___

Dear Steven,

   Thank you so much for helping with the landscaping project in front of City Hall. The area is far more eye-catching today than it was a week ago. You are a good worker and a dependable friend.

Special thanks,
Cody

Reference 69: Invitations

1.	What	– a special celebration luncheon
2.	Who	– for all the members of the Community Helpers Organization
3.	Where	– Community Center on Lighthouse Drive in Sherwood
4.	When	– on March 28, at 11:30
5.	Whipped Cream	– We hope you can come!

752 Firefly Road
Wichita, Kansas 70006
February 4, 20__

Dear Judy Morris,

You are cordially invited to a special celebration luncheon for all the members of the Community Helpers Organization. We will be honoring dedicated members who have actively changed the face of our community. The luncheon will be held on March 28, at the Community Center on Lighthouse Drive in Sherwood. We will begin serving lunch at 11:30. We hope you can come!

Sincerely,
Tina Woods

Student note: Notice that the five parts of an invitation are underlined in the example; however, you would not underline them in an actual invitation.

Reference 70: Parts of a Book

AT THE FRONT:

1. **Title Page.** This page has the full title of the book, the author's name, the illustrator's name, the name of the publishing company, and the city where the book was published.

2. **Copyright Page.** This page is right after the title page and tells the year in which the book was published and who owns the copyright. If the book has an ISBN number (International Standard Book Number), it is listed here.

3. **Preface** (also called **introduction**). If a book has this page, it will come before the table of contents and will usually tell you briefly why the book was written and what it is about.

4. **Table of Contents.** This section lists the major divisions of the book by units or chapters and tells their page numbers.

5. **Body.** This is the main section, or text, of the book.

AT THE BACK:

6. **Appendix.** This section includes extra informative material such as maps, charts, tables, diagrams, letters, etc. It is always wise to find out what is in the appendix, since it may contain supplementary material that you could otherwise find only by going to the library.

7. **Glossary.** This section is like a dictionary and gives the meanings of some of the important words in the book.

8. **Bibliography.** This section includes a list of books used by the author. It could serve as a guide for further reading on a topic.

9. **Index.** This will probably be your most useful section. The purpose of the index is to help you quickly locate information about the topics in the book. It has an alphabetical list of specific topics and tells on which page that information can be found. It is similar to the table of contents, but it is much more detailed.

Reference 71: Main Parts of the Library

Fiction Section
Fiction books contain stories about people, places, or things that are not true. Fiction books are arranged on the shelves in alphabetical order according to the authors' last names. Since fiction stories are made-up, they cannot be used when you research your report topic.

Non-Fiction Section
Non-Fiction books contain information and stories that are true.

Reference Section
The Reference Section is designed to help you find information on many topics. The Reference Section contains many different kinds of reference books and materials. Some of the ones that you need to know about will now be discussed.

- **Dictionary** (Reference Book)
  The dictionary gives the definition, spelling, pronunciation, and correct usage of words and tells briefly about famous people and places.

- **Encyclopedia** (Reference Book)
  The encyclopedia gives concise, accurate information about persons, places, and events of world-wide interest.

- **Atlas** (Reference Book)
  The atlas is primarily a book of maps, but it often contains facts about oceans, lakes, mountains, areas, population, products, and climates of every part of the world.

- **Almanac** (Reference Book)
  The World Almanac and *Information Please Almanac* are published once a year and contain brief, up-to-date information on a variety of topics.

- ***The Readers' Guide to Periodical Literature*** (Reference Book)
  The Readers' Guide to Periodical Literature is an index for magazines. It is a monthly booklet that lists the titles of articles, stories, and poems published in all leading magazines. These titles are listed under topics that are arranged alphabetically. The monthly issues of *The Readers' Guide to Periodical Literature* are bound together in a single volume once a year and filed in the library. By using the *Readers' Guide*, a person researching a topic can know which back issues of magazines might be helpful.

- **Card Catalog** (Reference File)
  The card catalog is a file of cards, arranged alphabetically, and usually placed in the drawers of a cabinet called the card catalog. It is an index to the library. Some libraries now have computer terminals that show the same information as the card catalog, but the information is stored in a computer. Often, the computer listing will also tell whether or not the book is currently on loan from the library.

Reference 72: Card Catalog Cards		
Author Card	**Title Card**	**Subject Card**
586.3	586.3	586.3
Author-Pacton, James R.	Title Science for Kids and	Topic Science Projects
Title Science for Kids and	Parents	Author-Pacton, James R.
Parents	Author-Pacton, James R.	Title Science for Kids and
Ill. by Charles Finley	Ill. by Charles Finley	Parents
Children's Press, Chicago	Children's Press, Chicago	Ill. by Charles Finley
(c1990) 116p.	(c1990) 116p.	Children's Press, Chicago
		(c1990) 116p.

Reference 73: Alphabetical Order

Example: Put each group of words in alphabetical order. Use numbers to show the order in each column.

Music Words		"B" Words		Math Words		Science Words		"T" Words	
2	1. guitar	**2**	3. barn	**2**	5. subtract	**2**	7. nucleus	**1**	9. tent
1	2. drums	**1**	4. bacon	**1**	6. multiply	**1**	8. neutron	**2**	10. test

---

Reference 74: Guide Words

Example: Below are the tops of two dictionary pages. Write the page number on which each word listed would appear.

decoration (first word)	Page 294	**deduct** (last word)		**deductible** (first word)	Page 295	**defense** (last word)

Page

294   1.   decoy

295   2.   deep

Reference 75: The Dictionary

1. The words listed in a dictionary are called entry words and are in bold face type.
2. The entry words are listed in alphabetical order (ABC order).
3. The dictionary tells how to spell the word and how to pronounce the word.
4. The dictionary tells what the word means and gives an example to explain the meaning.
5. The dictionary tells how to use the word and gives the part of speech for the word.

Entry Words

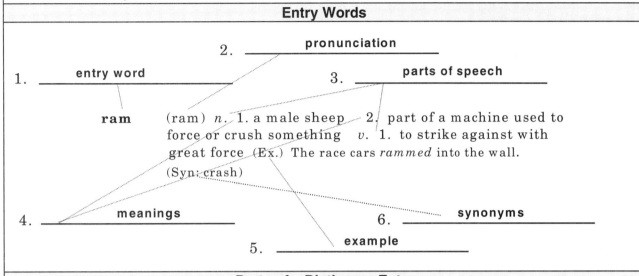

Parts of a Dictionary Entry

1. The entry word – gives correct spelling and divides the word into syllables.
2. Pronunciation – tells how to pronounce a word. It is usually put in parentheses.
3. Part of speech – uses small *n.* for noun, small *v.* for verb, *adj.* for adjective, etc.
4. Meanings – are numbered definitions listed according to the part of speech.
5. Example – a sentence using the entry word to illustrate a meaning. Shown as (Ex.)
6. Synonyms – words that have similar meanings to the entry word. Shown as (Syn:)

Reference 76: Outlines

Outline Guide	Sample Outline
Title	Fishing Trips
I. Introduction	I. Introduction

II. Main Topic (First main point)
   A. Subtopic (Supports first main point)
      1. Details (Supports subtopic)
      2. Details (Supports subtopic)
   B. Subtopic (Supports first main point)
   C. Subtopic (Supports first main point)
	II. Preparation
	   A. Gathering bait
	      1. Digging worms
	      2. Making dough balls
	   B. Checking the poles
	   C. Stocking the tackle box

III. Main Topic (Second main point)
   A. Subtopic (Supports second main point)
   B. Subtopic (Supports second main point)
	III. Departure
	   A. Fuel the car
	   B. Eat on the way

IV. Main Topic (Third main point)
   A. Subtopic (Supports third main point)
   B. Subtopic (Supports third main point)
	IV. Arrival
	   A. Baiting the hooks
	   B. Stringing the fish

V. Conclusion	V. Conclusion

Reference 77: Outline Information

First, an outline has a TITLE.

- At first, your outline title should be the same or similar to your narrowed topic. This will help you stay focused on the main idea of your report. If you decide to change the title for your final paper, you must remember to change your outline title.

- Capitalizing rules for titles are the same for outlines as for final papers: Capitalize the first word, the last word, and all the important words in between them. Conjunctions, articles, and prepositions with fewer than five letters are not usually capitalized unless they are the first or last word. Titles for reports are not underlined or placed in quotation marks unless the title is a quotation.

Second, an outline has Roman numerals denoting MAIN TOPICS.

- There must always be two or more Roman numerals. There can never be just one. For each Roman numeral, there is a paragraph. (Three Roman numerals - three paragraphs.)
- The information following a Roman numeral is called the main topic and gives the main idea, or main point, of each paragraph. It will be used to form the topic sentence of the paragraph.
- Every first word in a main topic is always capitalized.
- The periods after the Roman numerals must be lined up under each other.

Third, an outline has capital letters denoting SUBTOPICS.

- There must always be two or more capital letters. If you only have one, do not put it on the outline. Each capital letter is indented under the first word of the main topic.
- The information beside a capital letter is called the subtopic and gives details that support the main topic, or main point, of the paragraph.
- Every first word in a subtopic is always capitalized.
- The periods after the capital letters must be lined up under each other.

Fourth, an outline sometimes has Arabic numerals denoting DETAILS.

- There must always be two or more Arabic numerals. If you only have one, do not put it on the outline. Each Arabic numeral is indented under the first word of the subtopic.
- The information beside an Arabic numeral is called a detail and tells specific information about the subtopic of the paragraph.
- Every first word in a detail is always capitalized.
- The periods after the Arabic numerals must be lined up under each other.

Reference 78A: A Remarkable Person – Me

This activity produces a booklet about you. The instructions on how to make this booklet are given below. You will also be given directions on how to add artwork for each topic. Remember, this is a unique opportunity to express who you are at this stage of your life. This booklet would also make a wonderful gift to your parents, or you may save it and read it at different times as you grow older. You will certainly enjoy remembering what you were like as a fourth grader.

1. Have two sheets of construction paper. Use one sheet for the title page of your booklet and one sheet for the back cover.

2. Make a title page and illustrate it (or put a picture of yourself on it).

3. Make a separate page for each topic. Make each page special by doing some artwork for each topic. (*Example: Draw a big football and put "Goals for My Life" inside the football, and write your paragraph inside the football. You might want to add goal posts at the top and bottom of the page. Draw weights for "My Strengths," etc. Use creativity to match each topic with different kinds of artwork.*)

4. Do neat work.

5. Put the back cover on and staple your booklet on the left-hand side when you are finished. You can be proud of this booklet. No one else has one quite like it. It is an original, just like you!

(Title Page)	(Page 1)
A Booklet About A Remarkable Person **ME!** Written by (put your name here) Illustrated by (put your name here)	**Things I Like to Do** ...with a friend. ...with my family. ...by myself. ...that cost money. ...that are different. ...that are special.

Reference 78B: A Remarkable Person – Me	
(Page 2) Goals for My Life	(Page 3) Goals for the Rest of This School Year
(Page 4) My Strengths	(Page 5) My Weaknesses
(Page 6) My Special Feelings I am happy when... I am angry when... I hope that... I finally... I love... I admire... I want to be like... I get excited when... I need... I feel safe when... I am thankful for... I am afraid of... I feel sorry for... I am proud of... I am really good at...	(Page 7) My Family Other Special People

Reference 79: My Autobiography

Title: My Autobiography

Introductory sentence: My name is ___ ____ , and I am ____ years old.

I.   Family
    A.   Birth
    B.   Parents
    C.   Brothers and sisters
    D.   Grandparents

II.   Family life
    A.   Chores and responsibilities
    B.   How we celebrate special holidays
    C.   Family vacations
    D.   Special things about my family

III. School days
    A.   Friends
    B.   Teachers
    C.   Best/worst subjects
    D.   Special things about school

IV.   Special interests
    A.   Hobbies
    B.   My achievements
    C.   My likes and dislikes
    D.   Other

Notes

PRACTICE

SECTION

Chapter 1, Lesson 4, Practice: Write **a** or **an** in the blanks.

1. Did you find ____ answer yet?   4. We found ____ lost puppy.   7. ____ octopus   10. ____ light

2. We saw ____ icicle.   5. Mom ate ____ apple.   8. ____ friend   11. ____ ax

3. He ate ____ large steak.   6. I baked ____ pie.   9. ____ elevator   12. ____ box

---

Chapter 2, Lesson 5, Practice 1: Put the end mark and the abbreviation for each kind of sentence in the blanks.

1. Close your eyes and try to sleep   _____

2. Did you get new glasses   _____

3. I see the tornado   _____

4. I'm leaving on my trip tomorrow   _____

Chapter 2, Lesson 5, Practice 2

On notebook paper, write a sentence to demonstrate each of these four kinds of sentences:
(1) Declarative (2) Interrogative (3) Exclamatory (4) Imperative. Write the correct punctuation and the abbreviation that identifies it at the end. Use these abbreviations: **D, Int, E, Imp.**

Chapter 3, Lesson 3, Practice 1: Classify the sentence below. Underline the complete subject once and the complete predicate twice. Then, complete the table.

_____   The   pirate   ship   sailed   hastily   away.

List the Noun Used	List the Noun Job	Singular or Plural	Common or Proper	Simple Subject	Simple Predicate

---

Chapter 3, Lesson 3, Practice 2: Write **a** or **an** in the blanks.

1. She wore ____ blue dress.   4. He is ____ excellent cook.   7. ____ ear   10. ____ dream

2. I rode ____ motorcycle.   5. She is ____ active child.   8. ____ desk   11. ____ oven

3. They saw ____ elephant.   6. It was ____ new book.   9. ____ article   12. ____ swing

Chapter 3, Lesson 3, Practice 3

On notebook paper, write a sentence to demonstrate each of these four kinds of sentences:
(1) Declarative (2) Interrogative (3) Exclamatory (4) Imperative. Write the correct punctuation and
the abbreviation that identifies it at the end. Use these abbreviations: **D, Int, E, Imp.**

Chapter 3, Lesson 5, Practice Writing Page: Use the three-point outline form below to guide
you as you write a three-point expository paragraph.

Write a topic: _____

List 3 points about the topic:

1. _____ 2. _____ 3. _____

Sentence #1	Topic sentence (*Use words in the topic and tell how many points will be used.*)
Sentence #2	3-point sentence (*List your 3 points in the order that you will present them.*)
Sentence #3	State your first point in a complete sentence.
Sentence #4	Write a supporting sentence for the first point.
Sentence #5	State your second point in a complete sentence.
Sentence #6	Write a supporting sentence for the second point.
Sentence #7	State your third point in a complete sentence.
Sentence #8	Write a supporting sentence for the third point.
Sentence #9	Concluding sentence (*Restate the topic sentence and add an extra thought.*)

Student Note: Rewrite your nine-sentence paragraph on notebook paper. Be sure to indent and use the
checklists to help you edit your paragraph. Make sure you re-read your paragraph several times slowly.

Chapter 4, Lesson 1, Practice: Classify the sentence below. Underline the complete subject once and the complete predicate twice. Then, complete the table.

_____ The   feisty   poodle   strolled   proudly   away.

List the Noun Used	List the Noun Job	Singular or Plural	Common or Proper	Simple Subject	Simple Predicate

Finding One Part of Speech: For each sentence, write **SN** above the simple subject and **V** above the simple predicate. Underline the word(s) for the part of speech listed to the left of each sentence.

Adjective(s):   1. The crisp, crunchy candies disappeared quickly today.

Adverb(s):   2. The nervous young driver drove very safely away.

Noun(s):   3. The talented artist painted extremely well.

Adjective(s):   4. The canoe floated away.

Verb(s):   5. The academic team performed splendidly.

Chapter 4, Lesson 3, Practice: Put this 3-part assignment on notebook paper:

(1) Write the four parts of speech that you have studied so far (in any order).

(2) Write out the Question and Answer Flow in exact order for the sentence listed below.

(3) Classify the sentence.

Practice Sentence: Yesterday, the new youth minister preached fervently.

Chapter 6, Lesson 3, Practice: For each sentence, do these four things: (1) Write the subject. (2) Write **S** if the subject is singular or **P** if the subject is plural. (3) Write the rule number. (4) Underline the correct verb in the sentence.

Rule 1: A singular subject must use a singular verb form that ends in **s**: *is, was, has, does, or verbs ending with* **es**.

Rule 2: A plural subject, a compound subject, or the subject **YOU** must use a plural verb form that has **no s** ending: *are, were, do, have, or verbs without* **s** *or* **es** *endings.* (A plural verb form is also called the *plain form*.)

Subject	S or P	Rule	
			1. The parents (was, were) talking in the kitchen.
			2. Tim and John (is, are) good baseball players.
			3. My friend (was, were) drawing on the sidewalk with chalk.
			4. The driver (stop, stops) for the school bus.
			5. You (is, are) my best friend.
			6. They (was, were) swimming in the creek.
			7. He (rides, ride) without a saddle.
			8. The hunters (was, were) taken by surprise.
			9. John and Carol (is, are) working in the garden today.

Chapter 7, Lesson 1, Practice: For each sentence, do these four things: (1) Write the subject. (2) Write **S** if the subject is singular or **P** if the subject is plural. (3) Write the rule number. (4) Underline the correct verb in the sentence.

Rule 1: A singular subject must use a singular verb form that ends in **s**: *is, was, has, does, or verbs ending with* **es**.

Rule 2: A plural subject, a compound subject, or the subject **YOU** must use a plural verb form that has **no s** ending: *are, were, do, have, or verbs without* **s** *or* **es** *endings.* (A plural verb form is also called the *plain form.*)

Subject	S or P	Rule

1. The ducks (has, have) webbed feet.

2. Buffey (barks, bark) all night.

3. The cars in the parking lot (is, are) locked.

4. The flowers (grows, grow) fast during the summer.

5. You (is, are) doing a good job.

6. They (was, were) looking for a new pet.

7. She (goes, go) home every weekend.

8. The girls (was, were) working on a science project.

9. Bill and Joe (is, are) good friends.

10. (Was, Were) your keys in your pocket?

11. Our sled (was, were) sliding down the snowy hill.

12. (Do, Does) the football players run every day?

Chapter 10, Lesson 3, Practice: Use the Editing Guide below each sentence to know how many capitalization and punctuation errors to correct. For Sentence 1, write the capitalization and punctuation rule numbers for each correction in bold. For Sentence 2, write the capitalization and punctuation corrections. Use the capitalization and punctuation rule pages to help you.

1. I'll   be   home   on   Friday,   July   24   for   Mother's   birthday.

Editing Guide for Sentence 1: Capitals: 4   Commas: 1   Apostrophes: 2   End Marks: 1

2. my sister judy will serve lunch for mothers friends at caseys restaurant on saturday july 10

Editing Guide for Sentence 2: Capitals: 7   Commas: 3   Apostrophes: 2   End Marks: 1

Chapter 11, Lesson 1, Practice: Write the capitalization and punctuation rule numbers for each correction in bold.

3426 **T**aylor **C**ircle

Dallas, **T**exas 75224

August 23, 20—

Dear **B**illy,

    I have great news! **M**y father bought extra tickets to the **D**allas **C**owboys football game this

Saturday. **H**e said **I** could ask you to go with us! **W**e have seats on the fifty-yard line.

    My mom will call your parents about spending the weekend with me. **W**e'll have a great time!

I hope to see you soon.

Your pal,

John

Editing Guide: **Capitals: 20**   **Commas: 4**   **Apostrophes: 1**   **End Marks: 7**

Chapter 11, Lesson 2, Practice: Write the capitalization and punctuation corrections only.

176 buffalo trail

cody wyoming 24431

february 19 20—

dear cousin peggy

it doesnt seem possible that you and greg will be married twenty years in july are you going

to disney world in orlando florida i know it will be a long trip by car my family extends

congratulations do let us know about your trip

affectionately yours

andy

Editing Guide: Capitals: 21   Commas: 5   Apostrophes: 1   End Marks: 5

Chapter 12, Lesson 3, Practice: Find each error and write the correction above it. Write the punctuation corrections where they belong.

Highlighters and markers is writing instruments that have many things in common the most obveous is there felt tip and similar size. Both writing instruments use an felt tip to mark on a paige. Both writing instruments is larger than an regular pen or pencil. Finally, both writing instuments can be used to wright highlite, or color

Total Mistakes: 16

Chapter 13, Lesson 1, Practice 1: On notebook paper, add the part that is underlined in the parentheses to make each fragment into a complete sentence.

1. Beside the pool after lunch   (subject part, predicate part, <u>both the subject and predicate</u>)

2. Cooked and cleaned after the party   (<u>subject part</u>, predicate part, both the subject and predicate)

3. The funny little monkey at the zoo   (subject part, <u>predicate part</u>, both the subject and predicate)

Chapter 13, Lesson 1, Practice 2: Identify each kind of sentence by writing the abbreviation in the blank. **(S, F)**.

_____	1. The water churned rapidly.
_____	2. Above the sink in the bathroom and kitchen.
_____	3. The children ran happily to the playground.
_____	4. Signing his name to the document in the lawyer's office.
_____	5. The flat tire on the car in the middle of the road.

Chapter 13, Lesson 2, Practice 1: Put a slash to separate each run-on sentence below. Then, on notebook paper, correct the run-on sentences by rewriting them as indicated by the labels in parentheses at the end of each sentence.

1. Sam earned extra money he spent it on baseball cards. **(SCV)**

2. I am going to the library Jason is going to the library. **(SCS)**

3. My little puppy is very lovable he likes to play with me. **(SS)**

Chapter 13, Lesson 2, Practice 2: Identify each kind of sentence by writing the abbreviation in the blank. **(S, SS, F, SCS, SCV)**

_____	1. Whenever the peaches are ripe.
_____	2. My mother cooked the meal and served the guests.
_____	3. Cauliflower and broccoli are healthy foods.
_____	4. The tire went flat. Dad changed it.
_____	5. The invitation came in the mail.

Chapter 13, Lesson 3, Practice 1: Put a slash to separate each run-on sentence below. Then, on notebook paper, correct the run-on sentences by rewriting them as indicated by the labels in parentheses at the end of each sentence.

1. The cattle broke through the fence they grazed contentedly. (**SCV**)
2. The cattle broke through the fence they grazed contentedly. (**CD;**)
3. The cattle broke through the fence they grazed contentedly. (**CD, and**)
4. The cattle broke through the fence the sheep broke through also. (**SCS**)

Chapter 13, Lesson 3, Practice 2: Identify each kind of sentence by writing the abbreviation in the blank. (**S, F, SCS, SCV, CD**)

_____ 1. The dog growled and barked at the mailman.

_____ 2. David fixed the fence, and Teresa planted the flowers.

_____ 3. Her son and daughter were on the honor roll.

_____ 4. Crashed during the terrible storm.

_____ 5. I like classical music; my sister likes rock and roll.

Chapter 13, Lesson 3, Practice 3

On a sheet of notebook paper, write two compound sentences, using these labels to guide you:
① (CD, but) ② (CD;)

Chapter 14, Lesson 1, Practice 1: Choose an answer from the pronoun choices in parentheses. Fill in the other columns according to the titles. (**S** or **P** stands for singular or plural.)

Pronoun-antecedent agreement	Pronoun Choice	S or P	Antecedent	S or P
1. The speaker unbuttoned (his, their) jacket.				
2. Dad painted (his, their) truck yellow.				
3. My aunt lost (her, their) pet chicken.				
4. The protesters waved (his, their) flag.				
5. The vinegar lost (its, their) flavor.				

Chapter 14, Lesson 1, Practice 2: Identify each kind of sentence by writing the abbreviation in the blank. (**S, F, SCS, SCV, CD**)

_____ 1. She wrote a novel, but it has not been published.

_____ 2. Our aunt and uncle traveled to Europe with their friends.

_____ 3. In the cafeteria for two hours.

_____ 4. She washed the dishes for her mother.

_____ 5. Larry's brother rested and ate under the shade tree.

_____ 6. The sun came out, but it was still raining.

Chapter 14, Lesson 2, Practice 1: Choose an answer from the choices in parentheses. Fill in the other columns according to the titles. (**S or P** stands for singular or plural.)

Pronoun-antecedent agreement	Pronoun Choice	S or P	Antecedent	S or P
1. The student in the cafeteria lost (his, their) money.				
2. The apartments had no numbers on (it, them).				
3. The violinist played with (his, their) left hand.				
4. The boys invested (his, their) money in bonds.				
5. The tulip lost (its, their) petals suddenly.				
6. His sister lost (her, their) essay paper.				
7. The monkey made (its, their) bed with straw.				
8. The turtles buried (its, their) eggs in sand.				

Chapter 14, Lesson 2, Practice 2: Identify each kind of sentence by writing the abbreviation in the blank. (**S, F, SCS, SCV, CD**)

_____ 1. Since the interstate is closed to traffic.

_____ 2. The judge and jury agreed on the verdict.

_____ 3. I smelled the fire and called for help.

_____ 4. She ate her pancakes, but she was still hungry.

_____ 5. Seth entered and won the spelling contest.

_____ 6. I walked my dog, and I carried our cat.

_____ 7. In the bedroom on top of the dresser.

Chapter 14, Lesson 2, Practice 3

On notebook paper, write two compound sentences, using these labels to guide you:
①(**CD, but**) ② (**CD;**).

Chapter 14, Lesson 3, Practice 1: Choose an answer from the choices in parentheses. Fill in the other columns according to the titles. (**S or P** stands for singular or plural.)

Pronoun-antecedent agreement	Pronoun Choice	S or P	Antecedent	S or P
1. My nephew lives with (his, their) mother.				
2. The envelopes have no names on (it, them).				
3. The prince wore (his, their) royal robes.				
4. The young boy washed (his, their) hands.				
5. The nation struggled for (its, their) independence.				
6. The tourists left (its, their) luggage in the taxi.				
7. Sally wore (her, their) necklace to the prom.				
8. The bluebirds hatch (its, their) eggs in a box.				

Chapter 14, Lesson 3, Practice 2: Identify each kind of sentence by writing the abbreviation in the blank. (**S, F, SCS, SCV, CD**)

_____ 1. Where the brick wall used to stand.

_____ 2. The whales and sharks invaded the beach.

_____ 3. I answered the phone and listened to the recording.

_____ 4. My dog growled, but I petted him anyway.

_____ 5. The talented singer laughed and sang with the audience.

Chapter 15, Lesson 1, Practice: Part A: Underline each noun to be made possessive and write singular or plural (**S-P**), the rule number, and the possessive form.   Part B: Write each noun as singular possessive and then as plural possessive.

1. For a singular noun - add (**'s**)	2. For a plural noun that ends in **s** - add (**'**)	3. For a plural noun that does not end in **s** - add (**'s**)
Rule 1: boy's	**Rule 2: boys'**	**Rule 3: men's**

Part A	S-P	Rule	Possessive Form	Part B	Singular Possessive	Plural Possessive
1. hedge length				5. cousin		
2. donkeys tails				6. postman		
3. mirrors lengths				7. pirate		
4. women efforts				8. buggy		

Chapter 15, Lesson 2, Practice: Part A: Underline each noun to be made possessive and write singular or plural (**S-P**), the rule number, and the possessive form.   Part B: Write each noun as singular possessive and then as plural possessive.

1. For a singular noun - add (**'s**)	2. For a plural noun that ends in **s** - add (**'**)	3. For a plural noun that does not end in **s** - add (**'s**)
Rule 1: boy's	**Rule 2: boys'**	**Rule 3: men's**

Part A	S-P	Rule	Possessive Form	Part B	Singular Possessive	Plural Possessive
1. pigeons roosts				5. monkey		
2. children laughter				6. wife		
3. enemy surrender				7. child		
4. class decision				8. axle		

Chapter 15, Lesson 3, Practice: Part A: Underline each noun to be made possessive and write singular or plural (**S-P**), the rule number, and the possessive form. Part B: Write each noun as singular possessive and then as plural possessive.

1. For a singular noun - add (**'s**)		2. For a plural noun that ends in *s* - add (**'**)			3. For a plural noun that does not end in *s* - add (**'s**)	
Rule 1: girl's		**Rule 2: girls'**			**Rule 3: women's**	
Part A	**S-P**	**Rule**	**Possessive Form**	**Part B**	**Singular Possessive**	**Plural Possessive**
1. bike trail				5. baby		
2. wolves howls				6. ally		
3. women scarves				7. alley		
4. pantries shelves				8. scarf		

Chapter 16, Lesson 1, Practice 1: Part A: Underline each noun to be made possessive and write singular or plural (**S-P**), the rule number, and the possessive form. Part B: Write each noun as singular possessive and then as plural possessive.

1. For a singular noun - add (**'s**)		2. For a plural noun that ends in *s* - add (**'**)			3. For a plural noun that does not end in *s* - add (**'s**)	
Rule 1: girl's		**Rule 2: girls'**			**Rule 3: women's**	
Part A	**S-P**	**Rule**	**Possessive Form**	**Part B**	**Singular Possessive**	**Plural Possessive**
1. Ernie idea				5. man		
2. horse mane				6. diary		
3. Helen slipper				7. roof		
4. frogs skin				8. wolf		

Chapter 16, Lesson 1, Practice 2: Choose an answer from the pronoun choices in parentheses. Fill in the other columns according to the titles. (**S** or **P** stands for singular or plural.)

Pronoun-antecedent agreement	Pronoun Choice	S or P	Antecedent	S or P
1. The teacher asked the class to read to (her, them).				
2. My parents painted (his, their) barn yesterday.				
3. Connie admired her father and wrote about (her, him).				
4. Mom hugged Joe and gave (him, her) encouragement.				
5. The computers lost (its, their) connections.				

Chapter 16, Lesson 1, Practice 3: Identify each kind of sentence by writing the abbreviation in the blank. (**S, F, SCS, SCV, CD**)

_____ 1. She wrote a novel, but it has not been published.

_____ 2. Our aunt and uncle traveled to Europe with their friends.

_____ 3. In the cafeteria for two hours.

_____ 4. She washed the dishes for her mother.

_____ 5. Larry's brother rested and ate under the shade tree.

_____ 6. The sun came out, but it was still raining.

Chapter 16, Lesson 3, Practice: Part A: Underline each noun to be made possessive and write singular or plural (**S-P**), the rule number, and the possessive form. Part B: Write each noun as singular possessive and then as plural possessive.

1. For a singular noun - add (**'s**)				2. For a plural noun that ends in **s** - add (**'**)		3. For a plural noun that does not end in **s** - add (**'s**)	
Rule 1: girl's				**Rule 2: girls'**		**Rule 3: women's**	
Part A	**S-P**	**Rule**	**Possessive Form**	**Part B**		**Singular Possessive**	**Plural Possessive**
1. Sunday sermon				5. wife			
2. wolves howls				6. glossary			
3. Bill driveway				7. woman			
4. trucks tires				8. parent			

Chapter 17, Lesson 1, Practice: Use the Quotation Rules to help punctuate the quotations below. Underline the explanatory words.

1. governor   thompson   replied   this   is   our   final   offer

2. this   is   our   final   offer   governor   thompson   replied

3. after   the   christmas   play   i   exclaimed   barbara   good   job

4. barbara   good   job   i   exclaimed   after   the   christmas   play

Chapter 17, Lesson 2, Practice 1: Use the Quotation Rules to help punctuate the quotations below. Underline the explanatory words.

1. aunt   sarah   asked   will   you   close   the   door

2. will   you   close   the   door   asked   aunt   sarah

3. mother   said   take   the   trash   out   before   you   leave

Chapter 17, Lesson 2, Practice 2: Use the Quotation Rules to help punctuate the quotations below. Underline the explanatory words.

1. watch out for that bee roger yelled

2. how can i call you if your phone is out of order mandy asked

3. sally said i drove to oregon last september for a vacation

4. is your birthday in july or august michael inquired

Chapter 17, Lesson 2, Practice 3

On notebook paper, write three sentences, demonstrating each of the two quotations: Beginning quote and end quote.

Chapter 17, Lesson 3, Practice 1: Use the Quotation Rules to help punctuate the quotations below. Underline the explanatory words.

1. i will give you extra credit for your research paper on zig ziglars life said mrs smith

2. mrs smith said i will give you extra credit for your research paper on zig ziglars life

3. will you visit washington d c this summer with your family asked harry

4. harry asked will you visit washington d c this summer with your family

Chapter 17, Lesson 3, Practice 2

On notebook paper, write two sentences, demonstrating each of these two quotations: Beginning quote and end quote.

Chapter 18, Lesson 1, Practice: Identify each verb as regular or irregular by writing **R** or **I** in the first blank and the past tense form in the second blank. Also, underline each verb or verb phrase in sentences 5-9.

	Verb	R or I	Past Tense		Underline the Verb	R or I	Past Tense
1.	sting			5.	Gloria sits on the front row.		
2.	worry			6.	Donnie gnawed on the apple.		
3.	carve			7.	Marcie is singing in the choir.		
4.	wear			8.	Sam drives a new car.		
				9.	Clay loves model airplanes.		

Chapter 18, Lesson 2, Practice: Underline each verb or verb phrase. Identify the verb tense by writing a number **1** for present tense, a number **2** for past tense, or a number **3** for future tense. Write the past tense form and **R** or **I** for Regular or Irregular.

Verb Tense			Main Verb Past Tense Form	R or I
	1.	The paint had begun to peel.		
	2.	Julie is painting her nails.		
	3.	I am washing the car now.		
	4.	Tonight, we will stay at a motel.		
	5.	She has built a sand castle.		
	6.	Sheila will do the swan dive.		
	7.	Rhonda had written the poems.		
	8.	He carved his name in stone.		
	9.	We have driven all night.		

Chapter 18, Lesson 3, Practice 1: Underline each verb or verb phrase. Identify the verb tense by writing a number **1** for present tense, a number **2** for past tense, or a number **3** for future tense. Write the past tense form and **R** or **I** for Regular or Irregular.

Verb Tense			Main Verb Past Tense Form	R or I
	1.	The Coast Guard had rescued a ship.		
	2.	Will you adjust the margins?		
	3.	He will be writing a novel.		
	4.	I am defending myself in court.		

Chapter 18, Lesson 3, Practice 2: Change the underlined present tense verbs in Paragraph 1 to past tense verbs in Paragraph 2.

Paragraph 1: Present Tense

   My grandfather **raises** cattle. He **owns** a large farm in eastern Texas, and I **visit** him at least twice a year. I **help** him do chores around the farm. We **load** bags of grain onto the trailer and **ride** into the field to feed the cattle. We **tear** open the bags and **pour** the feed into a large feed trough for the cattle. Then, we **spray** their backs with fly repellant. When we **finish**, we **return** to the house for afternoon snacks and a tall glass of my grandmother's homemade lemonade. I **love** my grandfather and his farm!

Paragraph 2: Past Tense

   My grandfather _____ cattle. He _____ a large farm in eastern Texas, and

I _____ him at least twice a year. I _____ him do chores around the farm.

We _____ bags of grain onto the trailer and _____ into the field to feed the cattle.

We _____ open the bags and _____ the feed into a large feed trough for the cattle.

Then, we _____ their backs with fly repellant. When we _____,

we _____ to the house for afternoon snacks and a tall glass of my grandmother's

homemade lemonade. I _____ my grandfather and his farm!

Chapter 18, Lesson 3, Practice 3: Write the seven present tense helping verbs, the five past tense helping verbs, and the two future tense helping verbs.

Present Tense Helping Verbs	Past Tense Helping Verbs	Future Tense Helping Verbs
1. _____	1. _____	1. _____
2. _____	2. _____	2. _____
3. _____	3. _____	
4. _____	4. _____	
5. _____	5. _____	
6. _____		
7. _____		

Chapter 18, Lesson 3, Practice 4: Change the underlined mixed tense verbs in Paragraph 1 to present tense verbs in Paragraph 2.

Paragraph 1: Mixed Tenses

Cathy **watched** as the horses **prance** across the arena. The horses **held** their heads with such great elegance, and the riders **modeled** perfect riding posture. They **file** into a straight line and **wove** in and out of the obstacles. The lead rider **carries** a flag that he **left** on the final obstacle. As the horses **exited** the arena, the crowd **cheers** loudly. Cathy **closed** her eyes and **imagines** being the star of such a magnificent performance.

Paragraph 2: Present Tense

Cathy _____ as the horses _____ across the arena. The

horses _____ their heads with such great elegance, and the riders _____ perfect

riding posture. They _____ into a straight line and _____ in and out of the obstacles.

The lead rider _____ a flag that he _____ on the final obstacle. As the

horses _____ the arena, the crowd _____ loudly. Cathy _____ her

eyes and _____ being the star of such a magnificent performance.

Chapter 19, Lesson 2, Practice 1: Underline the negative words in each sentence. Rewrite each sentence on notebook paper and correct the double negative mistake as indicated by the rule number in parentheses at the end of the sentence.

Rule 1	Rule 2	Rule 3
Change the second negative to a positive.	Take out the negative part of a contraction.	Remove the first negative word (verb change).

1. There wasn't no sauce left. (Rule 1)

2. Julia doesn't have no sister. (Rule 3)

3. We don't see nothing in the box. (Rule 1)

4. Sally couldn't find no paint. (Rule 1)

5. John hadn't never climbed that hill. (Rule 2)

6. They didn't hear nothing about the test. (Rule 2)

7. Don't never miss your bus. (Rule 1)

8. The jury didn't have no questions. (Rule 3)

Chapter 19, Lesson 2, Practice 2: Underline each verb or verb phrase. Identify the verb tense by writing a number **1** for present tense, a number **2** for past tense, or a number **3** for future tense. Write the past tense form and **R** or **I** for Regular or Irregular.

Verb Tense		Main Verb Past Tense Form	R or I
	1. The boys are building a fort.		
	2. Did you swim in the pool?		
	3. The toddler has grown three inches.		
	4. I am cooking the meal.		
	5. I will be riding home with you.		
	6. Two monkeys swing on the tree vine.		
	7. We have skipped a report.		
	8. The lesson will begin at four o'clock.		

Chapter 19, Lesson 3, Practice 1: Copy the following **words** and **contractions** on notebook paper. Write the correct contraction beside each word; then, write the correct word beside each contraction.

Words: cannot, let us, do not, was not, they are, are not, had not, is not, she is, who is, you are, did not, it is, we are, were not, does not, has not, I am, I have, I had, will not, I will, would not, I would.

Contractions: he's, that's, you've, they've, he'd, she'd, he'll, we'll, we'd, they'd, shouldn't, couldn't.

Chapter 19, Lesson 3, Practice 2: Underline the negative words in each sentence. Rewrite each sentence on notebook paper and correct the double-negative mistake as indicated by the rule number in parentheses at the end of the sentence.

Rule 1	Rule 2	Rule 3
Change the second negative to a positive.	Take out the negative part of a contraction.	Remove the first negative word (verb change).

1. She couldn't find nothing in her desk. (Rule 2)

2. Doug hadn't never played basketball. (Rule 2)

3. They don't know nothing about it. (Rule 1)

4. He doesn't have no pets. (Rule 3)

5. There wasn't no time left. (Rule 1)

6. I didn't find no key. (Rule 3)

Chapter 19, Lesson 3, Practice 3: Underline each verb or verb phrase. Identify the verb tense by writing a number **1** for present tense, a number **2** for past tense, or a number **3** for future tense. Write the past tense form and **R** or **I** for Regular or Irregular.

Verb Tense		Main Verb Past Tense Form	R or I
	1. The pictures are falling off the walls.		
	2. The volunteers worked diligently.		
	3. She has called three times.		
	4. The church is changing locations.		
	5. The water will feel too cold.		

Chapter 20, Lesson 1, Practice 1: Underline each subject and fill in each column according to the title.

	List each Verb	Write PrN, PA, or None	Write L or A
1. Those pickles are sour.			
2. Our new home is beautiful.			
3. They rushed to the store.			
4. Panthers are fierce creatures.			
5. She is our new principal.			
6. All the glasses are dirty.			
7. That movie was very popular.			
8. Sally rode in the parade.			
9. They visited our school.			
10. Travis is a new student.			
11. My brother is riding his horse.			
12. Hudson is a small country town.			
13. The landscape was beautiful.			
14. Adam is the oldest child.			

Chapter 20, Lesson 1, Practice 2: Copy the following **words** and **contractions** on notebook paper. Write the correct contraction beside each word; then, write the correct word beside each contraction.

Words: he has, have not, we have, he had, you had, he will, they will, we would, they would, should not, could not, did not, he is, what is, he would, she has, has not, I am, you have, she had, will not, I will.

Contractions: I'm, it's, who's, aren't, you're, they're, wasn't, weren't, doesn't, didn't, can't, hasn't, won't.

Chapter 20, Lesson 2, Practice 1: Write the rule number from Reference 60 and the correct plural form of the nouns below.

		Rule	Plural Form			Rule	Plural Form
1.	pulley			6.	tax		
2.	wife			7.	studio		
3.	reef			8.	potato		
4.	moose			9.	trip		
5.	woman			10.	fly		

Chapter 20, Lesson 2, Practice 2: Underline each subject and fill in each column according to the title.

	List each Verb	Write PrN, PA, or None	Write L or A
1. Today is Friday.			
2. Our luggage was blue.			
3. The doctors went to Russia.			
4. Next month is December.			
5. Our campus is efficient.			
6. Anna is very polite.			
7. Samson was an excellent athlete.			
8. We bought her paintings.			
9. He went to Missouri.			
10. Those snakes are poisonous.			

Chapter 20, Lesson 2, Practice 3: Copy the following **words** and **contractions** on notebook paper. Write the correct contraction beside each word; then, write the correct word beside each contraction.

Words: that is, there is, they have, we had, they are, are not, had not, is not, she is, who is, you are.

Contractions: isn't, she's, what's, we're, don't, let's, he's, she's, haven't, I've, we've, you'd, we'd, I'll, I'd.

Chapter 20, Lesson 2, Practice 4

On notebook paper, write a beginning quote and an end quote. Underline the explanatory words.

Chapter 20, Lesson 3, Practice 1: Underline each subject and fill in each column according to the title.

	List each Verb	Write PrN, PA, or None	Write L or A
1. Spanish is a beautiful language.			
2. She washed her hands in the sink.			
3. The letters are slanted.			
4. The mouse ate the crumb.			
5. Those two boys are brothers.			
6. My muscles are sore.			

Chapter 20, Lesson 3, Practice 2: Write the rule number from Reference 60 and the correct plural form of the nouns below.

		Rule	Plural Form			Rule	Plural Form
1.	monkey			6.	fox		
2.	wharf			7.	stereo		
3.	spoof			8.	potato		
4.	fish			9.	author		
5.	man			10.	bully		

Chapter 20, Lesson 3, Practice 3: Underline the negative words in each sentence. Rewrite each sentence on notebook paper and correct the double negative mistake as indicated by the rule number in parentheses at the end of the sentence.

Rule 1	Rule 2	Rule 3
Change the second negative to a positive.	Take out the negative part of a contraction.	Remove the first negative word (verb change).

1. She didn't want nothing to eat. (Rule 1)

2. We hadn't never been to New York. (Rule 2)

3. She doesn't want no scholarships. (Rule 1)

4. The boys didn't catch no fish. (Rule 3)

Chapter 20, Lesson 3, Practice 4: Underline each verb or verb phrase. Identify the verb tense by writing a number **1** for present tense, a number **2** for past tense, or a number **3** for future tense. Write the past tense form and **R** or **I** for Regular or Irregular.

Verb Tense		Main Verb Past Tense Form	R or I
	1. Did you win the lottery?		
	2. They will rebuild the church.		
	3. In class, he was eating an apple.		
	4. I want a different truck.		

Chapter 20, Lesson 3, Practice 5: Copy the following **words** and **contractions** on notebook paper. Write the correct contraction beside each word; then, write the correct word beside each contraction.

Words: cannot, let us, do not, was not, they are, are not, had not, is not, she will, who is, you are.

Contractions: you'd, wouldn't, we're, can't, he'd, shouldn't, they're, who's, there's, she's, he's, I'd.

Chapter 21, Lesson 1, Practice

Use butcher paper, large pieces of construction paper, or poster board to make a colorful wall poster identifying the five parts of a friendly letter and the parts of an envelope. Write the title and an example for each of the five parts. Illustrate your work. Then, give an oral presentation about the friendly letter and the envelope when you have finished.

Chapter 21, Lesson 2, Practice

Write a friendly letter to a special friend or relative. Before you start, review the references and tips for writing friendly letters. After your letter has been edited, fold the letter and put it in an envelope. Address the envelope properly and mail it. Don't forget the stamp. (E-mail does not take the place of this assignment.)

Chapter 21, Lesson 3, Practice 1

On notebook paper, identify the parts of a friendly letter and envelope by writing the titles and an example for each title. Use References 63-64 to help you.

Chapter 21, Lesson 3, Practice 2

Write a friendly letter to a neighbor, nursing home resident, or relative. This person must be someone different from the person chosen in the previous lesson. Before you start, review the references and tips for writing friendly letters. After your letter has been edited, fold the letter and put it in an envelope. Address the envelope properly and mail it. Don't forget the stamp.

Chapter 22, Lesson 1, Practice

Use butcher paper, large pieces of construction paper, or poster board to make a colorful wall poster identifying the six parts of a business letter and the parts of a business envelope. Write the title and an example for each of the six parts of the business letter and envelope. Illustrate your work. Then, give an oral presentation about the business letter and the envelope when you have finished.

Chapter 22, Lesson 2, Practice 1

Write a friendly letter to a special friend or relative. Before you start, review the references and tips for writing friendly letters. After your letter has been edited, fold the letter and put it in an envelope. Address the envelope properly and mail it. Don't forget the stamp.

Chapter 22, Lesson 2, Practice 2

Write a business letter. You may invent the company and the situation for which you are writing. Before you begin, review the reasons for writing business letters and the four types of business letters (*Reference 65 on page 54*). After your letter has been edited, fold the letter and put it in an envelope. Address the envelope properly.

Chapter 22, Lesson 3, Practice 1

On notebook paper, identify the parts of a business letter and envelope by writing the titles and an example for each title. Use References 66 and 67 to help you.

Chapter 22, Lesson 3, Practice 2

Write a business letter. You may invent another company and the situation for which you are writing. Before you begin, review the reasons for writing business letters and the four types of business letters (*Reference 65*). This business must be different from the business chosen in the previous lesson. After your letter has been edited, fold the letter and put it in an envelope. Address the envelope properly.

Chapter 23, Lesson 1, Practice

Write your own thank-you note. First, think of a person who has done something nice for you or has given you a gift (*even the gift of time*). Next, write that person a thank-you note, using the information in the Reference Section as a guide.

Chapter 23, Lesson 2, Practice

Make your own invitation card. First, think of a special event or occasion and who will be invited. Next, make an invitation to send out, using the information in the Reference Section as a guide. Illustrate your card appropriately.

Chapter 23, Lesson 3, Practice 1: Match each part of a book listed below with the type of information it may give you. Write the appropriate letter in the blank. You may use each letter only once.

A. Title page	C. Index	E. Appendix
B. Copyright page	D. Bibliography	F. Glossary

1. _____ A list of books used by the author as references

2. _____ ISBN number

3. _____ Used to locate topics quickly

Chapter 23, Lesson 3, Practice 2: Match each part of a book listed below with the type of information it may give you. Write the appropriate letter in the blank. You may use each letter only once.

A. Title page	C. Copyright page	E. Bibliography	G. Body
B. Table of contents	D. Index	F. Preface	

1. _____ Exact page numbers for a particular topic

2. _____ Text of the book

3. _____ Reason the book was written

4. _____ Books listed for finding more information

Chapter 23, Lesson 3, Practice 3

On notebook paper, write the five parts found at the front of a book.

Chapter 23, Lesson 3, Practice 4

On notebook paper, write the four parts found at the back of a book.

Chapter 23, Lesson 3, Practice 5

Write the nine parts of a book on a poster and write a description beside each part. Illustrate and color the nine parts.

Chapter 24, Lesson 1, Practice 1: Underline the correct answers for numbers 1-3. Write the correct answers for numbers 4-5.

1. Biographies and autobiographies are arranged on the shelves in
   (**numerical order, alphabetical order**).

2. The main reference book that is primarily a book of maps is the
   (**encyclopedia, dictionary, atlas, almanac**).

3. The main reference book that is published once a year with a variety of up-to-date
   information is the   (**encyclopedia, dictionary, atlas, almanac**).

4. What would you find by going to *The Readers' Guide to Periodical Literature*?

   _____

5. What are the names of the three types of cards located in the card catalog?

   _____

Chapter 24, Lesson 1, Practice 2: Write True or False after each statement.

1. The title of the book is always the first line on each of the catalog cards.   _____

2. The *Readers' Guide to Periodical Literature* is an index to magazines.   _____

3. Biographies are arranged on the shelves according to the author's last name.   _____

4. The books in the nonfiction section are arranged numerically by a call number.   _____

5. Fiction and nonfiction books have numbers on their spines to locate them on a shelf.   _____

Chapter 24, Lesson 1, Practice 3

Select eight of your favorite fiction books and alphabetize them on notebook paper by the authors' last names.

Chapter 24, Lesson 1, Practice 4

Draw and label the three catalog cards for this book on a sheet of notebook paper: 822.14 *One Writer's Secret* by Andrea Paige, Thompson Press, Dallas, 1994, 264 p. (*About Emily Dickinson*).

Chapter 24, Lesson 2, Practice 1: Put each group of words in alphabetical order. Write numbers in the blanks to show the order in each column.

Car Words	Medical Words	"Q" Words	People Words	"V" Words
___ 1. hood	___ 7. cast	___ 13. quaint	___ 19. friends	___ 25. valley
___ 2. vents	___ 8. compress	___ 14. quote	___ 20. actors	___ 26. vibrant
___ 3. horn	___ 9. arteries	___ 15. quart	___ 21. heirs	___ 27. voice
___ 4. engine	___ 10. scapula	___ 16. quartz	___ 22. students	___ 28. vent
___ 5. brakes	___ 11. vaccine	___ 17. quest	___ 23. citizens	___ 29. victory
___ 6. wipers	___ 12. coronary	___ 18. queen	___ 24. sisters	___ 30. violet

Chapter 24, Lesson 2, Practice 2: Below are the tops of two dictionary pages. Write the page number on which each word listed would appear.

patriarch (first word)	Page 363	**pavilion** (last word)	**pedestrian** (first word)	Page 364	**penurious** (last word)

Page		**Page**		**Page**		**Page**	
___ 1. pedigree		___ 3. pelican		___ 5. pauper		___ 7. pennant	
___ 2. pattern		___ 4. penicillin		___ 6. pelts		___ 8. patrol	

Chapter 24, Lesson 3, Practice 1: Match the definitions of the parts of a dictionary entry below. Write the correct letter of the word beside each definition.

_____ 1. small *n.* for noun, small *v.* for verb, *adj.* for adjective, etc.	A. pronunciation
_____ 2. sentences using the entry word to illustrate a meaning	B. meanings
_____ 3. words that have similar meanings to the entry word	C. entry word
_____ 4. shows how to pronounce a word, usually put in parentheses	D. synonyms
_____ 5. correct spelling and divides the word into syllables	E. parts of speech
_____ 6. numbered definitions listed according to the part of speech	F. examples

Chapter 24, Lesson 3, Practice 2: Label each part of the dictionary entry below. Use the definitions in the matching exercise to help you.

2. _____

1. _____   3. _____

up•set (up set') *v.* 1. to interfere. 2. to knock over.
(Syn: spill) 3. to defeat unexpectedly. *adj.* 1. worried, anxious.
2. sick. (Ex.) Jane had an upset stomach after eating pizza.

6. _____   4. _____

5. _____

Chapter 24, Lesson 3, Practice 3: Write the meaning and the part of speech for each underlined word on the lines below.

	Word Meaning	**Part of Speech**
1. By accident, I <u>upset</u> the vase of flowers.	_____	_____
2. We were <u>upset</u> by the phone call.	_____	_____
3. Our team <u>upset</u> the champions.	_____	_____
4. Her <u>upset</u> stomach was the result of too many sweets.	_____	_____

Chapter 25, Lesson 1, Practice: Give an oral report on the main points of an outline that are given below. Make an outline as a visual aid to help in your presentation. *(You may use Reference 77 as your guide.)*

(1) Put periods after Roman numerals, capital letters, Arabic numerals, and any word that would require a period in a sentence.

(2) Capitalize the first word of each entry and any word that would be capitalized in a sentence.

(3) You cannot have a Roman numeral I. without a Roman numeral II., an A. without a B., or a 1. without a 2.

Chapter 25, Lesson 2, Practice: Copy the notes below into a two-point outline.

Notes   Outline

two types of summer jobs   _____

inside jobs   _____
grocery sackers
ticket takers   _____
outdoor jobs
landscaper   _____
lifeguard
                                               _____

                                               _____

                                               _____

Chapter 25, Lesson 3, Practice: Copy the notes below into a two-point outline.

Notes   Outline

two types of camping-out   _____

in the woods   _____
using a tent
using a camper   _____
at a motel
with air conditioning   _____
with room service
                                               _____

                                               _____

                                               _____

Notes

TEST

SECTION

Chapter 1 Test

Exercise 1: Identify each pair of words as synonyms or antonyms by putting parentheses ( ) around **syn** or **ant**. Write numbers 5 and 6 on notebook paper. For number 5, write two synonym words and identify them with **syn**. For number 6, write two antonym words and identify them with **ant**.

1. timid, bold	syn	ant	3. modest, forward	syn	ant	5.
2. slumber, sleep	syn	ant	4. depart, leave	syn	ant	6.

Exercise 2: Write **a** or **an** in the blanks.

1. We found _____ bird's nest.   4. We are _____ good team.   7. ____ eagle   10. ____ fur

2. They saw _____ odd bird.   5. It was _____ empty box.   8. ____ test   11. ____ orange

3. I have _____ awful cold.   6. He has _____ new friend.   9. ____ accident   12. ____ nose

Chapter 2 Test

Exercise 1: Match the definitions by writing the correct letter beside each numbered concept.

_____ 1. exclamatory sentence

_____ 2. a/an are also called

_____ 3. adjective modifies

_____ 4. verb question

_____ 5. a definite article

_____ 6. subject-noun question (thing)

_____ 7. article adjective can be called

_____ 8. makes a request or gives a command

_____ 9. noun

_____ 10. subject-noun question (person)

_____ 11. punctuation for declarative

_____ 12. adverb modifies

A. verb, adjective, or adverb

B. who

C. what is being said about

D. person, place, or thing

E. what

F. period

G. shows strong feeling

H. indefinite articles

I. noun or pronoun

J. the

K. noun marker

L. imperative sentence

Chapter 3 Test

Exercise 1: Classify each sentence.

1. _____ The four little cheerful toddlers laughed loudly.

2. _____ The huge scary ape walked suddenly away.

3. _____ The young baseball team played extremely well.

Exercise 2: Use Sentence 1 to underline the complete subject once and the complete predicate twice and to complete the table below.

List the Noun Used	List the Noun Job	Singular or Plural	Common or Proper	Simple Subject	Simple Predicate
1.	2.	3.	4.	5.	6.

Exercise 3: Identify each pair of words as synonyms or antonyms by putting parentheses ( ) around *syn* or *ant*.

1. implied, hinted	syn ant	3. precise, exact	syn ant	5. detest, admire	syn ant
2. idle, busy	syn ant	4. calamity, disaster	syn ant	6. aggression, retreat	syn ant

Exercise 4: Write *a* or *an* in the blanks.

1. We found _____ egg.   4. Did you see _____ eagle?   7. ____ pie   10. ____ airport

2. He wore _____ fancy costume. 5. I have _____ bad cold.   8. ____ churn   11. ____ anchovy

3. We ate _____ jelly donut.   6. I need _____ aspirin.   9. ____ echo   12. ____ game

Exercise 5: Match the definitions by writing the correct letter beside each numbered concept.

_____	1. tells what the subject does	A.	verb, adjective, or adverb
_____	2. a/an are also called	B.	what
_____	3. adjective modifies	C.	what is being said about?
_____	4. verb question	D.	person, place, or thing
_____	5. a definite article	E.	indefinite articles
_____	6. subject-noun question (thing)	F.	period
_____	7. article adjective can be called	G.	noun marker
_____	8. makes a request or gives a command	H.	who
_____	9. noun	I.	noun or pronoun
_____	10. subject-noun question (person)	J.	the
_____	11. punctuation for declarative	K.	verb
_____	12. adverb modifies	L.	imperative sentence

Exercise 6: On notebook paper, write one of each kind of the following sentences: Declarative, Interrogative, Exclamatory, Imperative. Write the punctuation and the abbreviation that identifies it at the end. Use these abbreviations: **D, Int, E, Imp.**

Exercise 7: In your journal, write a paragraph summarizing what you have learned this week.

Chapter 4 Test

Exercise 1: Classify each sentence.

1. _____ Today, the two hungry children ate rather quickly.

2. _____ The incredibly tall man stood up suddenly.

3. _____ The wise old owl looked piercingly everywhere.

Exercise 2: Use Sentence 2 to underline the complete subject once and the complete predicate twice and to complete the table below.

List the Noun Used	List the Noun Job	Singular or Plural	Common or Proper	Simple Subject	Simple Predicate
1.	2.	3.	4.	5.	6.

Exercise 3: Name the four parts of speech that you have studied so far.

1. _____ 2. _____ 3. _____ 4. _____

Exercise 4: Identify each pair of words as synonyms or antonyms by putting parentheses ( ) around *syn* or *ant*.

1. quiver, shake	syn ant	5. precise, exact	syn ant	9. implied, hinted	syn ant
2. vivid, dingy	syn ant	6. complicated, easy	syn ant	10. calamity, disaster	syn ant
3. admire, detest	syn ant	7. brawn, muscle	syn ant	11. delight, displease	syn ant
4. reply, answer	syn ant	8. idle, busy	syn ant	12. aggression, retreat	syn ant

Exercise 5: Write *a* or *an* in the blanks.

1. My friend lives in _____ igloo.　　3. Do you want _____ egg?　　5. _____ boot　7. _____ apology

2. He drove _____ new car.　　4. We need _____ vacation.　　6. _____ tree　8. _____ entertainer

Exercise 6: Match the definitions by writing the correct letter beside each numbered concept.

_____ 1. asks a question

_____ 2. a/an are also called

_____ 3. adjective modifies

_____ 4. the

_____ 5. subject question

_____ 6. article adjective can be called

_____ 7. makes a request or gives a command

_____ 8. noun

_____ 9. tells what the subject does

_____ 10. adverb modifies

A. verb, adjective, or adverb

B. a definite article

C. person, place, or thing

D. imperative sentence

E. indefinite articles

F. interrogative sentence

G. noun marker

H. who or what

I. noun or pronoun

J. verb

Exercise 7: On notebook paper, write one of each kind of the following sentences: Declarative, Interrogative, Exclamatory, Imperative. Write the punctuation and the abbreviation that identifies it at the end. Use these abbreviations: **D, Int, E, Imp.**

Exercise 8: In your journal, write a paragraph summarizing what you have learned this week.

Chapter 5 Test

Exercise 1: Classify each sentence.

1. _____ The explosive, fiery volcano on the mountainside erupted violently during the night!

2. _____ A keen, old mule deer stood still in the heavy thicket during hunting season.

3. _____ An expensive diamond necklace sparkled brightly through the window of the jewelry store.

Exercise 2: Use Sentence 3 to underline the complete subject once and the complete predicate twice and to complete the table below.

List the Noun Used	List the Noun Job	Singular or Plural	Common or Proper	Simple Subject	Simple Predicate
1.	2.	3.	4.	5.	6.
7.	8.	9.	10.		
11.	12.	13.	14.		

Exercise 3: Name the five parts of speech that you have studied. (*You may use abbreviations.*)

1. _____   2. _____   3. _____   4. _____   5. _____

Exercise 4: Identify each pair of words as synonyms or antonyms by putting parentheses ( ) around **syn** or **ant**.

1. pursue, follow	syn	ant	5. precise, exact	syn	ant	9. implied, hinted	syn	ant
2. proceed, cease	syn	ant	6. accept, reject	syn	ant	10. quiver, shake	syn	ant
3. brawn, muscle	syn	ant	7. tales, stories	syn	ant	11. delight, displease	syn	ant
4. reply, answer	syn	ant	8. vivid, dingy	syn	ant	12. aggression, retreat	syn	ant

Exercise 5: Write *a* or *an* in the blanks.

1. He whistled _____ happy tune.   3. It was _____ isolated event.   5. _____ quilt   7. _____ octopus

2. We saw _____ antelope.   4. They bought _____ big boat.   6. _____ fish   8. _____ instructor

Exercise 6: Match the definitions by writing the correct letter beside each numbered concept.

_____ 1. joins a noun or a pronoun to the rest of the sentence
_____ 2. a/an are also called
_____ 3. adjective modifies
_____ 4. noun or pronoun after a preposition
_____ 5. subject question
_____ 6. article adjective can be called
_____ 7. makes a request or gives a command
_____ 8. noun
_____ 9. tells what the subject does
_____ 10. adverb modifies

A. verb, adjective, or adverb
B. object of the preposition
C. person, place, or thing
D. imperative sentence
E. indefinite articles
F. preposition
G. noun marker
H. who or what
I. noun or pronoun
J. verb

Exercise 7: On notebook paper, write as many prepositions as you can.

Exercise 8: In your journal, write a paragraph summarizing what you have learned this week.

Chapter 6 Test

Exercise 1: Classify each sentence.

1. _____ Sit quietly at our kitchen table during your snack time after school.

2. _____ During the day, my pet frog sits on a large black rock in our little pond.

3. _____ We slept through the end of the midnight movie at her slumber party.

Exercise 2: Use Sentence 3 to underline the complete subject once and the complete predicate twice and to complete the table below.

List the Noun Used	List the Noun Job	Singular or Plural	Common or Proper	Simple Subject	Simple Predicate
1.	2.	3.	4.	5.	6.
7.	8.	9.	10.		
11.	12.	13.	14.		

Exercise 3: Name the six parts of speech that you have studied. (*You may use abbreviations.*)

1. _____   2. _____   3. _____   4. _____   5. _____   6. _____

Exercise 4: Identify each pair of words as synonyms or antonyms by putting parentheses ( ) around *syn* or *ant*.

1. vivid, dingy	syn	ant	5. arrange, prepare	syn	ant	9. pursue, follow	syn	ant
2. calm, turmoil	syn	ant	6. reply, answer	syn	ant	10. proceed, cease	syn	ant
3. idle, busy	syn	ant	7. tales, stories	syn	ant	11. accept, reject	syn	ant
4. soiled, dirty	syn	ant	8. belittle, encourage	syn	ant	12. delight, displease	syn	ant

Exercise 5: For each sentence, write the subject, then write **S** if the subject is singular or **P** if the subject is plural, write the rule number (*Rule 1 for singular or Rule 2 for plural*), and underline the correct verb in the sentence.

Rule 1: A singular subject must use a singular verb form that ends in **s**: *is, was, has, does, or verbs ending with* **s** *or* **es**.
Rule 2: A plural subject, a compound subject, or the subject **YOU** must use a plural verb form that has **no s** ending: *are, were, do, have, or verbs without* **s** *or* **es** *endings.* (A plural verb form is also called the *plain form*.)

Subject	S or P	Rule

1. My sister (was, were) singing in the school choir.

2. Jerry and Jeff (is, are) building a house.

3. The roads (has, have) many twists and turns.

4. That bush (need, needs) pruning today.

5. Some teachers (is, are) very strict.

6. My wrist (was, were) broken in the fall.

7. Horses (is, are) my favorite animals.

8. (Do, Does) those houses have numbers on them?

9. The garden (appear, appears) to be very plentiful.

10. The pilot (was, were) eager to land the plane.

Exercise 6: On notebook paper, write as many prepositions as you can.

Exercise 7: In your journal, write a paragraph summarizing what you have learned this week.

Chapter 7 Test

Exercise 1: Classify each sentence.

1. _____ My children stared breathlessly at the cows in Dad's pasture.

2. _____ Today, several duck eggs hatched slowly in the soft grass beside the edge of the pond.

3. _____ Stop by my favorite candy store in the mall on your way to our house.

Exercise 2: Use Sentence 1 to underline the complete subject once and the complete predicate twice and to complete the table below.

List the Noun Used	List the Noun Job	Singular or Plural	Common or Proper	Simple Subject	Simple Predicate
1.	2.	3.	4.	5.	6.
7.	8.	9.	10.		
11.	12.	13.	14.		

Exercise 3: Name the six parts of speech that you have studied. (*You may use abbreviations.*)

1. _____ 2. _____ 3. _____ 4. _____ 5. _____ 6. _____

Exercise 4: Identify each pair of words as synonyms or antonyms by putting parentheses ( ) around **syn** or **ant**.

1. soiled, dirty	syn ant	4. belittle, encourage	syn ant	7. arrange, prepare	syn ant
2. depress, uplift	syn ant	5. calm, turmoil	syn ant	8. fatigued, fresh	syn ant
3. brawn, muscle	syn ant	6. bucket, pail	syn ant	9. rival, competitor	syn ant

Exercise 5: Finding One Part of Speech. For each sentence, write **SN/SP** above the simple subject and **V** above the simple predicate. Underline the word(s) for the part of speech listed to the left of each sentence.

Adjective(s): 1. Our elementary teacher rode on my sister's brand-new motorcycle.

Preposition(s): 2. We carefully worked on the science project for the contest.

Pronoun(s): 3. I stayed at my sister's house during our family reunion.

Exercise 6: For each sentence, write the subject, then write **S** if the subject is singular or **P** if the subject is plural, write the rule number (*Rule 1 for singular or Rule 2 for plural*), and underline the correct verb in the sentence.

Subject	S or P	Rule

1. These people (know, knows) how to survive.
2. Beth and Gayle (is, are) this year's finalists.
3. The car (was, were) in need of gas.
4. You (was, were) two minutes too late.
5. (Doesn't, Don't) your uncle live in the red house?
6. (Do, Does) the residents still want city water?
7. My biscuits in the microwave (was, were) stale.
8. (Has, Have) Joan and her sisters stayed at the cabin?

Exercise 7: On notebook paper, write seven subject pronouns, seven possessive pronouns, and seven object pronouns.

Exercise 8: In your journal, write a paragraph summarizing what you have learned this week.

Chapter 8 Test

Exercise 1: Classify each sentence.

1. _____ Did the giraffe walk quietly by the children?

2. _____ Several pictures of my school could be seen in the paper.

3. _____ The three black bears have not returned to their den.

Exercise 2: Use Sentence 2 to underline the complete subject once and the complete predicate twice and to complete the table below.

List the Noun Used	List the Noun Job	Singular or Plural	Common or Proper	Simple Subject	Simple Predicate
1.	2.	3.	4.	5.	6.
7.	8.	9.	10.		
11.	12.	13.	14.		

Exercise 3: Name the six parts of speech that you have studied. (*You may use abbreviations.*)

1. _____   2. _____   3. _____   4. _____   5. _____   6. _____

Exercise 4: Identify each pair of words as synonyms or antonyms by putting parentheses ( ) around **syn** or **ant**.

1. implied, hinted	syn	ant	5. arrange, prepare	syn	ant	9. pursue, follow	syn	ant
2. keen, sharp	syn	ant	6. encourage, belittle	syn	ant	10. rival, competitor	syn	ant
3. admire, detest	syn	ant	7. pledge, promise	syn	ant	11. impetuous, cautious	syn	ant
4. calm, turmoil	syn	ant	8. unique, common	syn	ant	12. proceed, cease	syn	ant

Exercise 5: For each sentence, write the subject, then write **S** if the subject is singular or **P** if the subject is plural, write the rule number (*Rule 1 for singular or Rule 2 for plural*), and underline the correct verb in the sentence.

Subject	S or P	Rule

1. Chris (decides, decide) not to go.
2. Two windows (was, were) broken last night.
3. You (wasn't, weren't) home last night.
4. Brandon and Danny (has, have) left home.
5. His pup (is, are) on a leash.
6. The celery (is, are) covered with mold.
7. Wild violets (was, were) in bloom on the ridge.

Exercise 6: Finding One Part of Speech. For each sentence, write **SN/SP** above the simple subject and **V** (or **HV** and **V**) above the simple predicate. Underline the word(s) for the part of speech listed to the left of each sentence.

Noun(s):   1. At the beach, we swam in the water with our aunt.

Pronoun(s):   2. He will not advertise in her school newspaper.

Preposition(s):   3. After dark, we waded through the creek in our bare feet.

Exercise 7: In your journal, write a paragraph summarizing what you have learned this week.

Chapter 9 Test

Exercise 1: Classify each sentence.

1. _____ Look at all the broken branches on the ground after the severe storm.

2. _____ Whew! I studied for the annual spelling contest for six weeks!

3. _____ The nickel, quarter, and dime were minted in 1975.

Exercise 2: Use Sentence 2 to underline the complete subject once and the complete predicate twice and to complete the table below.

List the Noun Used	List the Noun Job	Singular or Plural	Common or Proper	Simple Subject	Simple Predicate
1.	2.	3.	4.	5.	6.
7.	8.	9.	10.		

Exercise 3: Name the eight parts of speech that you have studied. (*You may use abbreviations.*)

1. _____ 2. _____ 3. _____ 4. _____ 5. _____ 6. _____ 7. _____ 8. _____

Exercise 4: Answer each question below.

1. List the 8 **be** verbs. _____

2. What are the parts of a verb phrase? _____

3. Name the seven subject pronouns. _____

4. Name the seven possessive pronouns. _____

5. Name the seven object pronouns. _____

6. What part of speech is the word NOT? _____

Exercise 5: Identify each pair of words as synonyms or antonyms by putting parentheses ( ) around **syn** or **ant**.

1. bucket, pail	syn ant	5. hardy, robust	syn ant	9. pledge, promise	syn ant
2. rip, mend	syn ant	6. depress, uplift	syn ant	10. creeping, rushing	syn ant
3. fresh, fatigued	syn ant	7. unique, common	syn ant	11. sharp, keen	syn ant
4. soiled, dirty	syn ant	8. quill, feather	syn ant	12. impetuous, cautious	syn ant

Exercise 6: Underline the correct homonym in each sentence.

1. I really need some (coarse, course) sandpaper.

2. (Its, It's) a perfect day for a picnic.

3. I need (to, too, two) be absent tomorrow.

4. Look again at the (forth, fourth) question.

5. The (coarse, course) was too difficult for freshmen.

6. We traced the river to (its, it's) origin.

7. There are (to, too, two) rivers to cross in town.

8. She was (to, too, two) late for the appointment.

Exercise 7: In your journal, write a paragraph summarizing what you have learned this week.

Chapter 10 Test

Exercise 1: Classify each sentence.

1. _____ Droplets of water formed on the outside of her iced-tea glass.

2. _____ Ouch! My suspenders snapped tightly against my back!

3. _____ We have not studied or learned about fossils in our science class.

Exercise 2: Use Sentence 3 to underline the complete subject once and the complete predicate twice and to complete the table below.

List the Noun Used	List the Noun Job	Singular or Plural	Common or Proper	Simple Subject	Simple Predicate
1.	2.	3.	4.	5.	6.
7.	8.	9.	10.		

Exercise 3: Name the eight parts of speech that you have studied. (*You may use abbreviations.*)

1. _____   2. _____   3. _____   4. _____   5. _____   6. _____   7. _____   8. _____

Exercise 4: Identify each pair of words as synonyms or antonyms by putting parentheses ( ) around **syn** or **ant**.

1. pail, bucket	syn ant	5. difficult, complex	syn ant	9. tales, stories	syn ant
2. petite, large	syn ant	6. fatigued, fresh	syn ant	10. pledge, promise	syn ant
3. accept, reject	syn ant	7. commence, finish	syn ant	11. impetuous, cautious	syn ant
4. rude, impolite	syn ant	8. rival, competitor	syn ant	12. common, unique	syn ant

Exercise 5: Underline the correct homonym in each sentence.

1. She loves the (sent, scent) of fresh roses.
2. He (knew, new) the solution immediately.
3. Do you (know, no) the most direct route?
4. We (knew, new) he was not well.

5. Yesterday, Billy (sent, scent) Travis home.
6. Will you (right, write) your grandmother?
7. There is (know, no) excuse for his tardiness.
8. I drove a (knew, new) car today.

Exercise 6: Use the Editing Guide below each sentence to know how many capitalization and punctuation errors to correct. For Sentence 1, write the capitalization and punctuation rule numbers for each correction in bold. For Sentence 2, make the capitalization and punctuation corrections. Use the capitalization and punctuation rule pages to help you.

1. **Dr. S**mith's brother, **J**ohn, is a reporter for the **D**emocrat newspaper in **N**ew **Y**ork**.**

   Editing Guide: Capitals: 6   Commas: 2   Periods: 1   Apostrophes: 1   End Marks: 1

2. my brother and i went camping at yellowstone national park last friday saturday and sunday

   Editing Guide: Capitals: 8   Commas: 2   End Marks: 1

Exercise 7: In your journal, write a paragraph summarizing what you have learned this week.

Chapter 11 Test A

Exercise 1: <u>Sentence</u>: Write the capitalization and punctuation rule numbers for each correction in bold.

1. **H**is mother, **M**rs. **T. J. S**mith, owned an **I**talian restaurant near **D**allas, **T**exas.

Editing Guide: Capitals: 8	Commas: 3	Periods: 3	End Marks: 1

Exercise 2: <u>Friendly Letter</u>: Write the capitalization and punctuation corrections only.

500 crimson drive

chicago illinois 99542

may 18 20—

dear uncle jim

    thank you so much for the flowers you sent mom for mothers day they were arranged

perfectly in a beautiful vase mom was so surprised and happy to hear from you we look

forward to seeing you when you return from europe see you soon

your niece

teresa

Editing Guide: Capitals: 19	Commas: 4	Apostrophes: 1	End Marks: 5

Exercise 3: Name the eight parts of speech that you have studied. (*You may use abbreviations.*)

1. _____   2. _____   3. _____   4. _____   5. _____   6. _____   7. _____   8. _____

Exercise 4: Identify each pair of words as synonyms or antonyms by putting parentheses ( ) around **syn** or **ant**.

1. fiction, fable	syn ant	5. sharp, keen	syn ant	9. brawn, muscle	syn ant
2. uplift, depress	syn ant	6. complex, difficult	syn ant	10. creeping, rushing	syn ant
3. buy, auction	syn ant	7. silly, logical	syn ant	11. large, petite	syn ant
4. pause, hesitate	syn ant	8. feather, quill	syn ant	12. vivid, dingy	syn ant

Exercise 5: Underline the correct homonym in each sentence.

1. She writes on the prettiest (stationary, stationery).
2. Diplomats work hard to achieve (peace, piece).
3. The boy (threw, through) his shoes in the lake.
4. The train has been (stationary, stationery) for an hour.
5. I need a small (peace, piece) of chocolate.
6. He walked (threw, through) the hall alone.
7. What happened to (your, you're) hair?
8. I believe that (your, you're) a new student.

Exercise 6: In your journal, write a paragraph summarizing what you have learned this week.

Chapter 11 Test B

Exercise 1: Classify each sentence.

1. _____ The goldfish were swimming leisurely around the fish tank in my room.

2. _____ Read about current events in the daily newspaper.

3. _____ Our new baby sister is cooing and laughing at us now.

Exercise 2: <u>Sentence:</u> Write the capitalization and punctuation corrections only.

1. david sarah and i helped build a house in salt lake city utah for a destitute family

Editing Guide: Capitals: 7   Commas: 4   End Marks: 1

Exercise 3: <u>Friendly Letter:</u> Write the capitalization and punctuation rule numbers for each correction in bold.

12 **R**olling **H**ill **A**ve.

St. **P**aul, **M**innesota 72023

July 10, 20—

Dear **M**ike,

I won the state spelling bee last night. **M**s. **J**ames, my teacher, was so excited that she ran up on

the stage to congratulate me. **I** received a trophy and a $100 gift certificate. **M**y mom told me that

I'll now qualify for the national spelling bee in **W**ashington. **I** hope you can come. **W**rite soon.

Your cousin,

John

Editing Guide: Capitals: 20   Commas: 6   Periods: 3   Apostrophes: 1   End Marks: 6

Chapter 12 Test

Exercise 1: Classify each sentence.

1. _____ A powerful hurricane destroyed the beautiful white beaches near our resort!

2. _____ The story about the good Samaritan restored my faith in mankind.

3. _____ Good grief! We must seek shelter from this blistering sun!

Exercise 2: Use Sentence 3 to underline the complete subject once and the complete predicate twice and to complete the table below.

List the Noun Used	List the Noun Job	Singular or Plural	Common or Proper	Simple Subject	Simple Predicate
1.	2.	3.	4.	5.	6.
7.	8.	9.	10.		

Exercise 3: Identify each pair of words as synonyms or antonyms by putting parentheses ( ) around **syn** or **ant**.

1. endow, give	syn	ant	5. finish, commence	syn	ant	9. fiction, fable	syn	ant
2. agile, quick	syn	ant	6. demand, suggest	syn	ant	10. rival, competitor	syn	ant
3. hardy, robust	syn	ant	7. originates, begins	syn	ant	11. logical, silly	syn	ant
4. rip, mend	syn	ant	8. rude, impolite	syn	ant	12. delight, displease	syn	ant

Exercise 4: Underline the correct homonym in each sentence.

1. I will be gone for a (weak, week) or more.
2. Yesterday, she (lead, led) me to the kitchen.
3. He said he felt (weak, week) from the heat.
4. Did you (hear, here) the recess bell?
5. We have to use a number 2 (lead, led) pencil.
6. Put your coats over (hear, here), please.
7. Augusta is the (capital, capitol) of Maine.
8. Initials are written with (capital, capitol) letters.

Exercise 5: <u>For Sentences 1 and 2</u>: Write the capitalization and punctuation corrections only. <u>For Sentence 3</u>: Write the capitalization and punctuation rule numbers for each correction in bold.

1. holly did the swedish ambassador visit bangor maine on his way to the kennedy space center

Editing Guide: Capitals: 7   Commas: 3   End Marks: 1

2. today mr james and i visited a famous spanish mission called the alamo near san antonio

Editing Guide: Capitals: 8   Commas: 1   Periods: 1   End Marks: 1

3. Our captain, **Mr. R. J.** Nelson, showed us coral reefs in the **Atlantic Ocean** near **Greenwich, England.**

Editing Guide: Capitals: 9   Commas: 3   Periods: 3   End Marks: 1

Exercise 6: In your journal, write a paragraph summarizing what you have learned this week.

Chapter 13 Test

Exercise 1: Classify each sentence.

1. _____ The young man down the street mowed my lawn for a small fee.

2. _____ Mom and Dad ate lobster at the restaurant on their anniversary.

Exercise 2: Use Sentence 2 to underline the complete subject once and the complete predicate twice and to complete the table below.

List the Noun Used	List the Noun Job	Singular or Plural	Common or Proper	Simple Subject	Simple Predicate
1.	2.	3.	4.	5.	6.
7.	8.	9.	10.		
11.	12.	13.	14.		
15.	16.	17.	18.		
19.	20.	21.	22.		

Exercise 3: Identify each pair of words as synonyms or antonyms by putting parentheses ( ) around **syn** or **ant**.

1. conceal, hide	syn	ant	5. quill, feather	syn	ant	9. logical, silly	syn	ant
2. auction, buy	syn	ant	6. adhere, stick	syn	ant	10. pursue, follow	syn	ant
3. genuine, fake	syn	ant	7. creeping, rushing	syn	ant	11. gallant, afraid	syn	ant
4. hesitate, pause	syn	ant	8. quiver, shake	syn	ant	12. proceed, cease	syn	ant

Exercise 4: Put a slash to separate each run-on sentence below. Then, correct the run-on sentences by rewriting them on notebook paper as indicated by the labels in parentheses at the end of each sentence.

1. Dandelions are blooming they cover the yard. **(CD;)**

2. John whistled a tune Debbie whistled a tune. **(SCS)**

3. The boys put up a tent they slept outside. **(SCV)**

4. The student wrote a poem she read it to the class. **(CD**, and**)**

5. Todd launched the boat Ray helped him. **(SCS)**

6. She coughed uncontrollably she sneezed uncontrollably. **(SCV)**

Exercise 5: Identify each kind of sentence by writing the abbreviation in the blank. (**S, F, SCS, SCV, CD**).

_____ 1. Monkeys and tigers are my favorite animals at the zoo.

_____ 2. The house shook, and the pictures fell off the wall.

_____ 3. Walking along the beach during the summer.

_____ 4. The plumber turned off the water and replaced the copper tubing.

_____ 5. The young student ran to class, but he was late.

_____ 6. The detour through the country was very scenic.

_____ 7. She combs her hair, but she never brushes her teeth.

Exercise 6: On notebook paper, write one sentence for each of these labels: **(S) (SCS) (SCV) (CD)**.

Exercise 7: In your journal, write a paragraph summarizing what you have learned this week.

Chapter 14 Test

Exercise 1: Classify each sentence.

1. _____   I   traced   and   copied   a   picture   of   a   horse   during   my   art   class.

2. _____   Our   troops   invaded   and   occupied   the   enemy's   territory.

Exercise 2: Use Sentence 2 to underline the complete subject once and the complete predicate twice and to complete the table below.

List the Noun Used	List the Noun Job	Singular or Plural	Common or Proper	Simple Subject	Simple Predicate
1.	2.	3.	4.	5.	6.
7.	8.	9.	10.		

Exercise 3: Identify each pair of words as synonyms or antonyms by putting parentheses ( ) around **syn** or **ant**.

1. quick, agile	syn ant	5. bashful, shy	syn ant	9. originates, begins	syn ant
2. flashy, plain	syn ant	6. endow, give	syn ant	10. treaty, agreement	syn ant
3. demand, suggest	syn ant	7. gallant, afraid	syn ant	11. complex, difficult	syn ant
4. mend, rip	syn ant	8. hardy, robust	syn ant	12. emerge, disappear	syn ant

Exercise 4: Choose an answer from the choices in parentheses. Fill in the other columns according to the titles. (**S or P** stands for singular or plural.)

Pronoun-antecedent agreement

	Pronoun Choice	S or P	Antecedent	S or P
1. The ships at sea have changed (its, their) course.				
2. The small country won (its, their) independence.				
3. The Sunday school teachers lost (his, their) lesson.				
4. The doctor's wife misplaced (her, their) purse.				
5. The wild pheasant lost (its, their) tail feathers.				
6. The students in school brought (his, their) permission slip.				

Exercise 5: Identify each kind of sentence by writing the abbreviation in the blank. (**S, F, SCS, SCV, CD**)

_____ 1. Take your medicine, or you'll never get well.

_____ 2. I walked along the sandy beach.

_____ 3. The teachers and students cheered for our football team.

_____ 4. After lunch on Saturday.

_____ 5. She never studies, but she makes good grades.

_____ 6. My sister cooked and cleaned our house today.

_____ 7. During the storm last night.

Exercise 6: On notebook paper, write one sentence for each of these labels: (**S**) (**SCS**) (**SCV**) (**CD**).

Exercise 7: In your journal, write a paragraph summarizing what you have learned this week.

Chapter 15 Test

Exercise 1: Classify each sentence.

1. _____ My grandmother waters the flowers in her yard during the summer months.

2. _____ The small child would not eat the honeycomb from the beehive.

Exercise 2: Use Sentence 1 to underline the complete subject once and the complete predicate twice and to complete the table below.

List the Noun Used	List the Noun Job	Singular or Plural	Common or Proper	Simple Subject	Simple Predicate
1.	2.	3.	4.	5.	6.
7.	8.	9.	10.		
11.	12.	13.	14.		
15.	16.	17.	18.		

Exercise 3: Identify each pair of words as synonyms or antonyms by putting parentheses ( ) around **syn** or **ant**.

1. fable, fiction	syn	ant	5. rude, impolite	syn	ant	9. emerge, disappear	syn	ant
2. hesitate, pause	syn	ant	6. deplore, approve	syn	ant	10. creeping, rushing	syn	ant
3. hope, despair	syn	ant	7. genuine, fake	syn	ant	11. delicious, tasty	syn	ant
4. conceal, hide	syn	ant	8. sway, influence	syn	ant	12. petite, large	syn	ant

Exercise 4: Part A: Underline each noun to be made possessive and write singular or plural (**S-P**), the rule number, and the possessive form. Part B: Write each noun as singular possessive and then as plural possessive.

1. For a singular noun - add (**'s**)			2. For a plural noun that ends in **s** - add (**'**)			3. For a plural noun that does not end in **s** - add (**'s**)		
Rule 1: girl's			**Rule 2: girls'**			**Rule 3: women's**		
Part A	**S-P**	**Rule**	**Possessive Form**		**Part B**	**Singular Poss**	**Plural Poss**	
1. tractor warranty					12. knife			
2. actors roles					13. saddle			
3. oxen yokes					14. penny			
4. lemon rind					15. woman			
5. men wives					16. monkey			
6. Jessie address					17. captain			
7. roses thorns					18. child			
8. patients rights					19. parrot			
9. curtain design					20. party			
10. wives closets					21. wolf			
11. children concerns					22. radio			

Exercise 5: On notebook paper, write one sentence for each of these labels: **(S) (SCS) (SCV) (CD)**.

Exercise 6: In your journal, write a paragraph summarizing what you have learned this week.

Chapter 16 Test

Exercise 1: Classify each sentence.

1. ________ Play us a song on your new electric piano.

2. ________ I bought you several new shoes with the special discounts from the shoe store.

3. ________ Did the curator give your group an informative tour of the museum?

Exercise 2: Use Sentence 3 to underline the complete subject once and the complete predicate twice and to complete the table below.

List the Noun Used	List the Noun Job	Singular or Plural	Common or Proper	Simple Subject	Simple Predicate
1.	2.	3.	4.	5.	6.
7.	8.	9.	10.		
11.	12.	13.	14.		
15.	16.	17.	18.		

Exercise 3: Identify each pair of words as synonyms or antonyms by putting parentheses **( )** around ***syn*** or ***ant***.

1. adhere, stick	syn ant	5. auction, buy	syn ant	9. delicious, tasty	syn ant
2. petty, important	syn ant	6. drought, flood	syn ant	10. finish, commence	syn ant
3. mock, mimic	syn ant	7. flashy, plain	syn ant	11. treaty, agreement	syn ant
4. bashful, shy	syn ant	8. nervous, uneasy	syn ant	12. impetuous, cautious	syn ant

Exercise 4: Underline the correct homonym in each sentence.

1. We (knew, new) better than to refuse.
2. (Their, There, They're) is the new student.
3. Your perfume has an odd (sent, scent).
4. I wonder if (their, there, they're) still going.
5. The store on the corner is (knew, new).
6. I like (their, there, they're) new swing.

Exercise 5: Identify each kind of sentence by writing the abbreviation in the blank. **(S, F, SCS, SCV, CD)**

__________ 1. Beside the workbench in your dad's garage.
__________ 2. The cat and dog played together.
__________ 3. Kim researched and typed her essay.
__________ 4. I went to the beach, but I never got in the water.

Exercise 6: Part A: Underline each noun to be made possessive and write singular or plural (**S-P**), the rule number, and the possessive form. Part B: Write each noun as singular possessive and then as plural possessive.

Rule 1: boy's		Rule 2: boys'		Rule 3: men's		
Part A	**S-P**	**Rule**	**Possessive Form**	**Part B**	**Singular Poss**	**Plural Poss**
1. Edgar homer				5. wife		
2. officer badge				6. fly		
3. Kent suitcase				7. dairy		
4. patients rights				8. deer		

Exercise 7: In your journal, write a paragraph summarizing what you have learned this week.

Chapter 17 Test

Exercise 1: Classify each sentence.

1. _____ Give Clint and Craig a copy of a United States map for their report.

2. _____ Jennifer's parents loaned her the money for a new car.

Exercise 2: Use Sentence 2 to underline the complete subject once and the complete predicate twice and to complete the table below.

List the Noun Used	List the Noun Job	Singular or Plural	Common or Proper	Simple Subject	Simple Predicate
1.	2.	3.	4.	5.	6.
7.	8.	9.	10.		
11.	12.	13.	14.		

Exercise 3: Identify each pair of words as synonyms or antonyms by putting parentheses ( ) around **syn** or **ant**.

1. praise, commend	syn ant	5. sway, influence	syn ant	9. adhere, stick	syn ant
2. deplore, approve	syn ant	6. hope, despair	syn ant	10. flimsy, sturdy	syn ant
3. gallant, afraid	syn ant	7. neutral, biased	syn ant	11. originates, begins	syn ant
4. youth, young	syn ant	8. give, endow	syn ant	12. suggest, demand	syn ant

Exercise 4: Use the Quotation Rules to help punctuate the quotations below. Underline the explanatory words.

1. did you get a part-time job after school i asked beth

2. beth answered i work three days a week at smiths shoe store

3. is it hard to work and go to school i inquired

4. beth stated proudly i get straight a s and i like the extra money

Exercise 5: On notebook paper, write one sentence for each of these labels: **(S) (SCS) (SCV) (CD)**.

Exercise 6: On notebook paper, write two sentences, demonstrating each of these two quotations: Beginning quote and end quote.

Exercise 7: In your journal, write a paragraph summarizing what you have learned this week.

Chapter 18A Test

Exercise 1: Classify each sentence.

1. _____ Wow! My best friend sent me a present from her hometown in Uruguay!

2. _____ Did you make your grandparents a card for their anniversary in your art class?

Exercise 2: Use Sentence 2 to underline the complete subject once and the complete predicate twice and to complete the table below.

List the Noun Used	List the Noun Job	Singular or Plural	Common or Proper	Simple Subject	Simple Predicate
1.	2.	3.	4.	5.	6.
7.	8.	9.	10.		
11.	12.	13.	14.		
15.	16.	17.	18.		

Exercise 3: Identify each pair of words as synonyms or antonyms by putting parentheses ( ) around **syn** or **ant**.

1. mock, mimic	syn ant	5. peril, danger	syn ant	9. error, wrong	syn ant
2. bicker, agree	syn ant	6. flimsy, sturdy	syn ant	10. escalate, decrease	syn ant
3. genuine, fake	syn ant	7. petty, important	syn ant	11. hardy, robust	syn ant
4. agile, quick	syn ant	8. youth, young	syn ant	12. conceal, hide	syn ant

Exercise 4: Underline each verb or verb phrase. Identify the verb tense by writing a number **1** for present tense, a number **2** for past tense, or a number **3** for future tense. Write the past tense form and **R** or **I** for Regular or Irregular.

Verb Tense		Main Verb Past Tense Form	R or I
	1. She is moving to an apartment.		
	2. The caller will leave a message.		
	3. Was she washing the windows?		
	4. The cattle are wading in the creek.		
	5. The coach had instructed his players.		
	6. Kim will eat the strawberries.		
	7. I pretended not to see.		
	8. They have built bonfires before.		
	9. Stuart is leaving for home.		
	10. He was running very fast.		

Exercise 5: Identify each kind of sentence by writing the abbreviation in the blank. (**S, F, SCS, SCV, CD**)

_____ 1. She collected seashells, and her brother sold them.

_____ 2. We stopped for a hamburger and were on our way.

_____ 3. The cowboy and his dogs herded the cattle.

_____ 4. Besides the cost of shipping.

_____ 5. The actor missed his cue, and we all laughed.

Exercise 6: Change the underlined present tense verbs in Paragraph 1 to past tense verbs in Paragraph 2.

Paragraph 1: Present Tense

I **crawl** into bed and **reach** for my favorite book. I **snuggle** under my covers and **open** my book. Reading **is** an adventure for me. The story **comes** alive as I **read**. My heart **pounds** as the mystery **builds**. I **sniff** and **wipe** my eyes at the sad or romantic scenes. Reading **is** better than a movie! Finally, my eyes no longer **stay** open. I **sigh** and **close** my book. Reluctantly, I **turn** off the light and **continue** my reading adventures in my dreams!

Paragraph 2: Past Tense

I _____ into bed and _____ for my favorite book. I _____ under my covers and _____ my book. Reading _____ an adventure for me. The story _____ alive as I _____. My heart _____ as the mystery _____. I _____ and _____ my eyes at the sad or romantic scenes. Reading _____ better than a movie! Finally, my eyes no longer _____ open. I _____ and _____ my book. Reluctantly, I _____ off the light and _____ my reading adventures in my dreams!

Exercise 7: Change the underlined mixed tense verbs in Paragraph 1 to present tense verbs in Paragraph 2.

Paragraph 1: Mixed Tense

I **open** my jewelry box and **gasped**. My grandmother's gold necklace **is** not there! I **was** frantic! I **move** everything off my desk and anxiously **searched** for my grandmother's heirloom. I **looked** under my bed and in my closet. Finally, I **sat** on the bed, and tears of frustration **fill** my eyes. Suddenly, my daughter **walked** into my room with my grandmother's gold necklace around her neck. She **hugged** me and **thanks** me for the loan of the necklace. She **was wearing** it to the antique banquet!

Paragraph 2: Present Tense

I _____ my jewelry box and _____. My grandmother's gold necklace _____ not there! I _____ frantic! I _____ everything off my desk and anxiously _____ for my grandmother's heirloom. I _____ under my bed and in my closet. Finally, I _____ on the bed, and tears of frustration _____ my eyes. Suddenly, my daughter _____ into my room with my grandmother's gold necklace around her neck. She _____ me and _____ me for the loan of the necklace. She _____ _____ it to the antique banquet!

Exercise 8: On notebook paper, write one sentence for each of these labels: **(S) (SCS) (SCV) (CD)**.

Exercise 9: On notebook paper, write two sentences, demonstrating each of the two kinds of quotations: Beginning quote and end quote.

Exercise 10: On notebook paper, write the seven present tense helping verbs, the five past tense helping verbs, and the two future tense helping verbs.

Exercise 11: In your journal, write a paragraph summarizing what you have learned this week.

Chapter 19 Test

Exercise 1: Classify each sentence.

1. _____ Go with us to the museum on Friday.

2. _____ Our mother gave daily piano lessons to the children in our neighborhood.

3. _____ My little sister's new shoes gave her terrible blisters on her feet.

Exercise 2: Identify each pair of words as synonyms or antonyms by putting parentheses ( ) around **syn** or **ant**.

1. remain, stay	syn	ant	5. hope, despair	syn	ant	9. sway, influence	syn	ant
2. drought, flood	syn	ant	6. biased, neutral	syn	ant	10. dim, bright	syn	ant
3. praise, commend	syn	ant	7. connect, separate	syn	ant	11. uneasy, nervous	syn	ant
4. shy, bashful	syn	ant	8. puzzle, mystery	syn	ant	12. emerge, disappear	syn	ant

Exercise 3: Change the underlined mixed tense verbs in Paragraph 1 to past tense verbs in Paragraph 2.

Paragraph 1: Mixed Tenses

The weather **was** hot, and the builders **are** tired. The thermometer **read** well above one hundred degrees. The sweat from the builders' foreheads **dripped** down their cheeks and **streaks** their dusty faces. Their water jugs **are** almost empty, and it **is** only mid-afternoon. The tired workers **send** a young crew member to refill the coolers. Before he **returned**, the neighborhood children **offer** the men several pitchers of ice-cold lemonade. The thirsty builders **smile** blissfully as they **guzzled** down the sweet treat.

Paragraph 2: Past Tense

The weather _____ hot, and the builders _____ tired. The thermometer _____ well above one hundred degrees. The sweat from the builders' foreheads _____ down their cheeks and _____ their dusty faces. Their water jugs _____ almost empty, and it _____ only mid-afternoon. The tired workers _____ a young crew member to refill the coolers. Before he _____, the neighborhood children _____ the men several pitchers of ice-cold lemonade. The thirsty builders _____ blissfully as they _____ down the sweet treat.

Exercise 4: Copy the following words on notebook paper. Write the correct contraction beside each word. Words: you have, there is, is not, they will, will not, it is, he will, let us, we would, I will, you will, was not, do not, they have, I am, does not, have not.

Exercise 5: Copy the following contractions on notebook paper. Write the correct word beside each contraction. Contractions: they're, he's, you're, hasn't, you'd, we've, doesn't, hadn't, can't, I'd, don't.

Exercise 6: Write the seven present tense helping verbs, the five past tense helping verbs, and the two future tense helping verbs on notebook paper.

Exercise 7: In your journal, write a paragraph summarizing what you have learned this week.

Chapter 20 Test

Exercise 1: Classify each sentence.

1. _____ Julie's grandmother gave her a tender hug before the ceremony.

2. _____ My brother and I yelled wildly and raced frantically after the departing bus!

Exercise 2: Identify each pair of words as synonyms or antonyms by putting parentheses ( ) around **syn** or **ant**.

1. bicker, agree	syn	ant	4. escalate, decrease	syn	ant	7. peril, danger	syn	ant
2. dwell, live	syn	ant	5. allow, forbid	syn	ant	8. wrong, error	syn	ant
3. flashy, plain	syn	ant	6. blunder, mistake	syn	ant	9. subordinate, leader	syn	ant

Exercise 3: Underline each subject and fill in each column according to the title.

1. A wedding gown is expensive.
2. Giants have big feet.
3. Rhode Island is the smallest state.
4. Florida is a peninsula.
5. Beets are very healthy.
6. The chef prepared a fine dessert.

List each Verb	Write PrN, PA, or None	Write L or A

Exercise 4: Write the rule number from Reference 60 and the correct plural form of the nouns below.

		Rule	Plural Form				Rule	Plural Form
1.	donkey				6.	church		
2.	doily				7.	ox		
3.	louse				8.	fish		
4.	patio				9.	half		
5.	wife				10.	bluff		

Exercise 5: Underline the negative words in each sentence. Rewrite each sentence on notebook paper and correct the double negative mistake as indicated by the rule number in parentheses at the end of the sentence.

Rule 1	Rule 2	Rule 3
Change the second negative to a positive.	Take out the negative part of a contraction.	Remove the first negative word (verb change).

1. The pen doesn't have no ink. (Rule 3)
2. My goldfish wouldn't eat no food. (Rule 2)
3. Paul didn't want no bread. (Rule 1)
4. The driver didn't never change lanes. (Rule 3)
5. This recipe doesn't call for no sugar. (Rule 1)
6. I wouldn't never repeat that. (Rule 2)

Exercise 6: Copy the following words on notebook paper. Write the correct contraction beside each word.
Words: cannot, let us, do not, was not, they are, are not, had not, is not, she is, who is, you are, did not, it is.

Exercise 7: In your journal, write a paragraph summarizing what you have learned this week.

Chapter 21 Test

Exercise 1: Classify each sentence.

1. _____ The green apples gave me a terrible pain in my stomach yesterday.

2. _____ My brother and I picked wild berries in the woods behind our house.

Exercise 2: Identify each pair of words as synonyms or antonyms by putting parentheses ( ) around **syn** or **ant**.

1. oppose, agree	syn	ant	4. degrade, praise	syn	ant	7. endow, give	syn	ant
2. neutral, biased	syn	ant	5. safe, secure	syn	ant	8. shame, dishonor	syn	ant
3. terror, fear	syn	ant	6. clutter, order	syn	ant	9. compete, cooperate	syn	ant

Exercise 3: Choose an answer from the choices in parentheses. Then, fill in the rest of the columns according to the titles. (**S** or **P** stands for singular or plural.)

Pronoun-antecedent agreement

Pronoun Choice	S or P	Antecedent	S or P

1. I think the farmer has lost (his, their) cows.

2. The entrance with (its, their) flashing lights was beautiful.

3. Both turtles have lost (its, their) shells.

4. Her sandals needed (its, their) straps tightened.

5. The wind lost (its, their) intensity after the storm.

6. The bubbles made (its, their) way to the clouds.

7. My tooth has (its, their) root exposed.

Exercise 4: Write the rule number from Reference 60 and the correct plural form of the nouns below.

		Rule	Plural Form				Rule	Plural Form
1.	key				6.	box		
2.	holly				7.	child		
3.	mouse				8.	deer		
4.	radio				9.	knife		
5.	leaf				10.	cliff		

Exercise 5: Write the seven present tense helping verbs, the five past tense helping verbs, and the two future tense helping verbs.

Exercise 6: Copy the following words on notebook paper. Write the correct contraction beside each word. Words: cannot, let us, do not, was not, they are, are not, had not, is not, she is, who is, you are, did not, it is, we are, were not, does not, has not, I am, I have, I had or I would, will not, I will, would not, should not, could not, they would.

Exercise 7: On notebook paper, identify the parts of a friendly letter and envelope by writing the titles and an example for each title. Use References 63 and 64 to help you.

Exercise 8: In your journal, write a paragraph summarizing what you have learned this week.

Chapter 22 Test

Exercise 1: Classify each sentence.

1._____ The red schooner raced through the choppy water on the lake today.

2._____ Roger and Tina sell their handmade woven baskets at the fall festival.

Exercise 2: Identify each pair of words as synonyms or antonyms by putting parentheses ( ) around **syn** or **ant**.

1. innocent, guilty	syn	ant	4. compete, cooperate	syn	ant	7. safe, secure	syn	ant
2. connect, separate	syn	ant	5. retain, remember	syn	ant	8. terror, fear	syn	ant
3. stern, hard	syn	ant	6. clutter, order	syn	ant	9. harshness, sweetness	syn	ant

Exercise 3: Use the Quotation Rules to help punctuate the quotations below. Underline the explanatory words.

1. nancy do you want to go to blackwood mall tomorrow asked katherine

2. kevin shouted loudly to amy and amber look out for that power line

3. i would like to see susans new dress shop today kimberly said to her mother

4. the new employee stated boldly i would like to work the evening shift if possible mr davis

5. that bull is going to trample the cowboy gasped julie to her brother

Exercise 4: On notebook paper, identify the parts of a business letter and envelope by writing the titles and an example for each title. Use References 66 and 67 to help you.

Exercise 5: On notebook paper, identify the parts of a friendly letter and envelope by writing the titles and an example for each title. Use References 63 and 64 to help you.

Exercise 6: On notebook paper, write one sentence for each of these labels: **(S) (SCS) (SCV) (CD)**.

Exercise 7: On notebook paper, write the seven present tense helping verbs, the five past tense helping verbs, and the two future tense helping verbs.

Exercise 8: In your journal, write a paragraph summarizing what you have learned this week.

Chapter 23 Test

Exercise 1: Classify each sentence.

1. _____ The lovely bluebonnet flowers cover the prairies in parts of Texas.

2. _____ Ellen talked and laughed with her sister for an hour on the phone.

Exercise 2: Match each part of a book listed below with the type of information it may give you. Write the appropriate letter in the blank. You may use each letter only once.

A. Title page	B. Copyright page	C. Index	D. Bibliography	E. Appendix	F. Glossary

1. ___ A list of books used by the author as references

2. ___ Meanings of important words in the book

3. ___ Publisher's name and city where the book was published

4. ___ ISBN number

5. ___ Used to locate topics quickly

6. ___ Extra maps in a book

Exercise 3: Match each part of a book listed below with the type of information it may give you. Write the appropriate letter in the blank. You may use each letter only once.

A. Title page	C. Copyright page	E. Bibliography	G. Body
B. Table of contents	D. Index	F. Preface	

1. ___ Exact page numbers for a particular topic

2. ___ Author's name, title of book, and illustrator's name

3. ___ Books listed for finding more information

4. ___ Text of the book

5. ___ Reason the book was written

6. ___ Titles of units and chapters

7. ___ Copyright date

Exercise 4: On notebook paper, write the five parts found at the front of a book.

Exercise 5: On notebook paper, write the four parts found at the back of a book.

Exercise 6: Write a thank-you note. First, think of a person who has done something nice for you or has given you a gift (even the gift of time). Next, write that person a thank-you note, using the information in the Reference Section as a guide.

Exercise 7: Make an invitation card. First, think of a special event or occasion and who will be invited. Next, make an invitation to send out, using the information in the Reference Section as a guide. Illustrate your card appropriately.

Exercise 8: In your journal, write a paragraph summarizing what you have learned this week.

Chapter 24A Test

Exercise 1: Classify each sentence.

1. _____ Jason stacked the wood by the porch.

2. _____ An eyewitness gave the police a description of the criminal.

Exercise 2: Put each group of words in alphabetical order. Use numbers to show the order in each column.

Animal Words	Month Words	"B" Words	Car Words	"L" Words
____ 1. hamster	____ 5. July	____ 9. blunder	____ 13. muffler	____ 17. laughter
____ 2. baboon	____ 6. August	____ 10. bull	____ 14. bumper	____ 18. llama
____ 3. skunk	____ 7. April	____ 11. brazen	____ 15. tailpipe	____ 19. livery
____ 4. guinea	____ 8. October	____ 12. buffalo	____ 16. generator	____ 20. licorice

Exercise 3: Below are the tops of two dictionary pages. Write the page number on which each word listed would appear.

floor (first word)	Page 178	**fluid** (last word)

focus (first word)	Page 179	**footstool** (last word)

Page		**Page**		**Page**		**Page**	
_____	1. flour	_____	3. foliage	_____	5. folklore	_____	7. folksy
_____	2. food	_____	4. flourish	_____	6. football	_____	8. flop

Exercise 4: Match the definitions of the parts of a dictionary entry below. Write the correct letter of the word beside each definition.

_____ 1. small *n.* for noun, small *v.* for verb, *adj.* for adjective, etc. A. pronunciation

_____ 2. sentences using the entry word to illustrate a meaning B. meanings

_____ 3. words that have similar meanings to the entry word C. entry word

_____ 4. shows how to pronounce a word, usually put in parentheses D. synonyms

_____ 5. correct spelling and divides the word into syllables E. parts of speech

_____ 6. numbered definitions listed according to the part of speech F. examples

Chapter 24B Test

Exercise 5: Underline the correct answer for numbers 1-5. Write the correct answers for numbers 6-7.

1. Nonfiction books are arranged on the shelves in (**numerical order, alphabetical order**).

2. Fiction books are arranged on the shelves in (**numerical order, alphabetical order**).

3. The main reference book that is primarily a book of maps is the
   (**encyclopedia, dictionary, atlas, almanac**).

4. The main reference book that gives the definition, spelling, and pronunciation of words is the
   (**encyclopedia, dictionary, atlas, almanac**).

5. The main reference book that is published once a year with a variety of up-to-date information is the
   (**encyclopedia, dictionary, atlas, almanac**).

6. What would you find by going to *The Readers' Guide to Periodical Literature*?

   _____

7. What are the names of the three types of cards located in the card catalog?

   _____

Exercise 6: Put the fiction books below in the correct order to go on the shelves. Write numbers 1-4 in the blanks to show the correct order. *(Alphabetize fiction books by authors' last names.)*

1. *Ulysses* by James Joyce   _____

2. *The Old Man and the Sea* by Ernest Hemingway   _____

3. *Now in November* by Josephine Johnson   _____

4. *The Scarlet Letter* by Nathaniel Hawthorne   _____

Exercise 7: Write True or False for each statement.

1. Fiction and nonfiction books have numbers on their spines to locate them on a shelf.   _____

2. The title of the book is always the first line on each of the catalog cards.   _____

3. The books in the fiction section are arranged alphabetically by the author's last name.   _____

4. The *Readers' Guide to Periodical Literature* is an index to magazines.   _____

5. Biographies are arranged on the shelves according to the author's last name.   _____

6. The books in the nonfiction section are arranged numerically by a call number.   _____

Exercise 8: Draw and label the three types of catalog cards for this book on notebook paper: 833.6 *Writers on Writing* by Charles Tyndall, Fulton Press, Houston, 1997, 265p. *(Use the catalog card examples in Reference 72.)*

Exercise 9: In your journal, write a paragraph summarizing what you have learned this week.

Chapter 25 Test

Exercise 1: Classify each sentence.

1. _____ The girls and boys on the debate team competed for the first-place trophy.

2. _____ The cowboys chase and lasso the runaway calves at the ranch.

3. _____ My parents gave me a lecture about bicycle helmets and safety.

Exercise 2: Copy the notes below into a two-point outline.

Notes	Outline
preparing for exams	_____
studying alone	_____
reviewing class notes	
skimming headlines	_____
studying with others	_____
rap sessions	
oral quizzes	_____
	_____
	_____
	_____

Exercise 3: On notebook paper, write all the jingles that you can recall from memory. There is a total of 17.

Exercise 4: In your journal, write a paragraph summarizing what you have learned this week.

Notes